WordPerfect® Version 6 for Windows™ First Run

LoriLee Sadler
Indiana University, Bloomington

WordPerfect Version 6 for Windows First Run

Copyright © 1994 by Que® Corporation.

Library of Congress Catalog No.: 93-86970

ISBN: 1-56529-430-0

97   96   95   94   4   3   2   1

Interpretation of the printing code: the rightmost double-digit number is the year of the book's printing; the rightmost single-digit number, the number of the book's printing. For example, a printing code of 94-1 shows that the first printing of the book occurred in 1994.

Screens reproduced in this book were created using Collage Plus from Inner Media, Inc., Hollis, NH.

WordPerfect Version 6 for Windows First Run is based on WordPerfect 6.0 for Windows.

Publisher: David P. Ewing

Associate Publisher: Paul Boger

Director of Editing & Operations: Chris Katsaropoulos

Book Designer: Amy Peppler-Adams

Production Team: Stephen Adams, Angela Bannan, Karen Dodson, Bob LaRoche, Elizabeth Lewis, Andrea Marcum, G. Alan Palmore, Nanci Sears Perry, Linda Quigley, Beth Rago, Suzanne Tully, Lillian Yates

About the Author

LoriLee Sadler teaches introductory computer courses, using both IBM and Macintosh computers, to more than 1,700 students each year at Indiana University. Since 1989, she has designed and developed curricula for noncomputer science majors and worked with other computer science faculty to create a computing program for nonmajors; this program is being used as a model at many large universities. In January 1993, Sadler took a senior administrative position as the pedagogical expert in the Associate Vice President's Office for Information Technology. She continues to teach in the department of computer science. She is the author of *MS-DOS SmartStart*, *Lotus 1-2-3 First Run*, and *WordPerfect 5.1 First Run*, all published by Que College, and is coauthor of three Macintosh applications texts. LoriLee Sadler holds a B.A. from Northeast Missouri State University, and an M.A. from Indiana University.

Editorial Director
Carol Crowell

Series Editor
M.T. Cozzola Cagnina

Managing Editor
Sheila B. Cunningham

Editorial Coordinator
Elizabeth D. Brown

Composed in *Garamond* and *MCPdigital* by Que Corporation

Table of Contents

Acknowledgments

It is virtually impossible to write a book of this nature without a great deal of help from others. I offer my sincere thanks to Sheila Cunningham for taking the time to carefully read, edit, and read again the chapters in this text. I also would like to thank the author of the Que College textbook, *WordPerfect Version 6 for Windows SmartStart*, Samantha Penrod of Purdue University, Calumet.

Que College is grateful for the assistance provided by the following reviewers: Ralph Duffy, North Seattle Community College and Jean Insinga, of Middlesex Community College. A special thanks also to our technical editor, Lynda Michele Reader, College of DuPage.

Trademarks

All terms mentioned in this book that are known to be trademarks or service marks have been appropriately capitalized. Que cannot attest to the accuracy of this information. Use of a term in this book should not be regarded as affecting the validity of any trademark or service mark.

Microsoft, Microsoft Excel, and MS-DOS are registered trademarks, and Windows is a trademark of Microsoft Corporation. WordPerfect is a registered trademark of WordPerfect Corporation. IBM is a registered trademark of International Business Machines Corporation. 1-2-3 and Lotus are registered trademarks of Lotus Development Corporation.

Preface

The *First Run* series is designed for the novice computer user who wants to learn the basics of a software application as quickly as possible.

First Run combines practical explanations of new concepts and hands-on steps and exercises to build proficiency quickly. Each *First Run* is organized into an average of ten Teaching Units. Each Teaching Unit teaches an important skill set. The objectives that make up each Teaching Unit build on one another section by section. Within each section are steps for performing the function or using the feature, plus an exercise to build your skills. Definitions of new terms and notes on working more effectively also are included.

First Run also offers Testing Your Skills sections to enable an instructor to evaluate progress. A Glossary of terms is included in every book.

Each section in a unit takes an average of 15 minutes to complete. Since each exercise is tied directly to the current section, instructors can instantly determine a student's progress before continuing to the next section.

An *Instructor's Resource Disk* is available upon adoption of the textbook. It contains answers to all of the exercises in the textbook, as well as suggested lecture notes, additional teaching tips and information, extra optional exercises, completed data files, and other data files used in the course.

The unique combination of features in this concise guide makes *First Run* an ideal textbook for step-by-step teaching now and for easy reference later on. Instructors may mix and match individual textbooks in order to design a custom software applications course.

Look for the following additional titles in the First Run series:

BASIC First Run	1-56529-416-5
dBASE IV First Run	1-56529-419-X
Excel for Windows First Run	1-56529-420-3
Introduction to PCs First Run	1-56529-417-3
Lotus 1-2-3 Release 2.x First Run (covers 2.4 and below)	1-56529-421-1
MS-DOS First Run	1-56529-423-8
Novell NetWare First Run	1-56529-424-6
Windows 3.1 First Run	1-56529-425-4
WordPerfect 5.1 First Run	1-56529-428-9
WordPerfect 6 First Run	1-56529-429-7

For more information call

1-800-428-5331

or contact your local Que College Representative

Conventions Used in This Book

Certain conventions are used throughout the text and graphics of *WordPerfect Version 6 for Windows First Run*.

References to keys are as they appear on the keyboard of the IBM Personal Computer and most IBM-compatibles: ⏎Enter. When two keys appear together, for example, ⇧Shift+F2, you press and hold down the first key as you also press the second key.

Menu letters that you type to activate a command appear in boldface, for example, **F**ile. Messages and exact quotations from the computer screen are printed in a `special typeface`.

Getting Started

1

This unit covers the basics of using WordPerfect for Windows: starting the program, understanding the layout of the WordPerfect for Windows screen, and making selections from pull-down menus. The procedures for changing directories and exiting the program are also presented.

1.1: To Start WordPerfect for Windows

In order to use WordPerfect for Windows, you must operate it from within the Windows program (the graphical user interface). WordPerfect for Windows can be started in three ways:

- From the Windows WordPerfect for Windows icon
- From the Windows Program Manager's File menu
- From the DOS system prompt

Unit 1: Getting Started

The following examples assume that you have successfully installed WordPerfect for Windows on your hard drive.

STEPS To start WordPerfect for Windows by using the Windows icon, follow these steps:

1. Start Windows at the C:\> prompt in DOS by typing **win** and pressing ⏎Enter.

   The Program Manager window appears, displaying the program icons.

2. Double-click the WPWIN60 icon to display the WordPerfect for Windows group of icons.

3. Double-click the WPWIN60 icon within the group to open the WordPerfect for Windows program.

STEPS To start WordPerfect for Windows from the Program Manager File menu, follow these steps:

1. Start Windows at the C:\> prompt in DOS by typing **win** and pressing ⏎Enter.

   The Program Manager window appears.

2. Open the File menu.

3. From the File menu, choose the **Run** command.

   The Run dialog box appears with the insertion point flashing in the Command Line text box (see fig. 1.1).

4. Type **wpwin.exe** and press ⏎Enter.

   NOTE You may need to type the complete path for the location of the WordPerfect for Windows program if the statement in your AUTOEXEC.BAT was not updated when the program was installed. For example, instead of typing **wpwin.exe**, type **c:\wpwin60\wpwin.exe**, and press ⏎Enter.

Fig. 1.1
The Run dialog box.

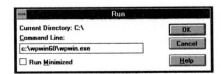

To start WordPerfect for Windows from the DOS system prompt, follow
these steps:

STEPS

1. Make sure that the correct subdirectory is displayed at the DOS system
   prompt, for example C:\wpwin60.

2. Type **win wpwin**, and press ⏎Enter.

Exercise 1: Starting WordPerfect for Windows

In this exercise you will start WordPerfect for Windows using one of the three
methods described above.

1. Boot your computer, if necessary.

2. Using one of the methods described above, start WordPerfect for
   Windows.

3. A new blank WordPerfect document will be presented on-screen,
   as shown in figure 1.2.

4. You will continue to work with this open document in subsequent
   exercises.

1.2: To Identify the Parts of the WordPerfect for Windows Screen

The WordPerfect program window appears full-size when you start the
program. The WordPerfect window contains the following components
(see fig. 1.2):

- **Title bar**
- **Menu bar**
- **Power bar**
- **Document window** with horizontal and vertical scroll bars
- **Status bar**

WordPerfect also contains two optional components which you can display in
the WordPerfect window: the *Button bar* and the *Ruler bar*.

Fig. 1.2
The full-size WordPerfect program window you see when you start the program.

Title Bar displays the program name and name of current (active) document.

Program Control menu is used to display commands to move or resize the WordPerfect program window, access the Program Manager in Windows, or close the WordPerfect program window and exit WordPerfect.

Document Control menu is used to restore, move, size, minimize, maximize, close, or edit the next open document.

Menu bar provides access to various pull-down menus, which contain commands for the topic shown on the Menu bar.

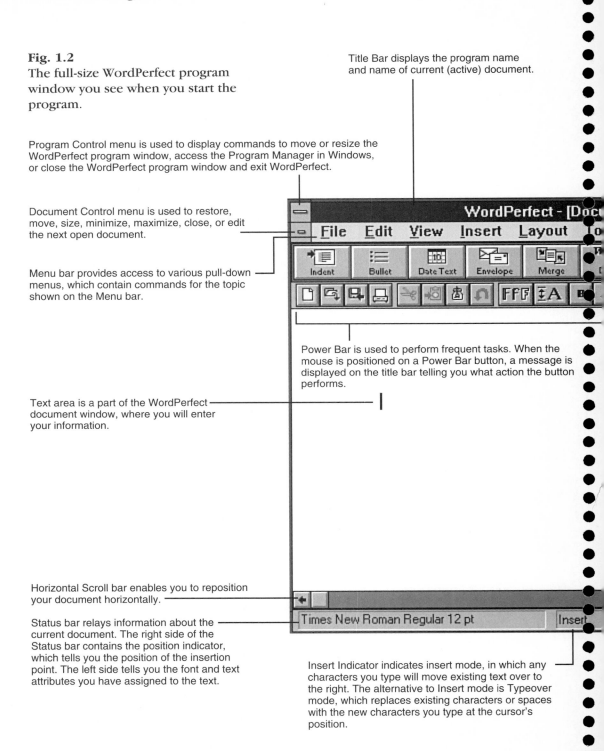

Power Bar is used to perform frequent tasks. When the mouse is positioned on a Power Bar button, a message is displayed on the title bar telling you what action the button performs.

Text area is a part of the WordPerfect document window, where you will enter your information.

Horizontal Scroll bar enables you to reposition your document horizontally.

Status bar relays information about the current document. The right side of the Status bar contains the position indicator, which tells you the position of the insertion point. The left side tells you the font and text attributes you have assigned to the text.

Insert Indicator indicates insert mode, in which any characters you type will move existing text over to the right. The alternative to Insert mode is Typeover mode, which replaces existing characters or spaces with the new characters you type at the cursor's position.

To Identify the Parts of the WordPerfect for Windows Screen

Minimize button shrinks the WordPerfect program to an icon at the bottom of the Windows desktop. Even though the program is still running (still loaded in main memory), it no longer uses the full display screen.

Restore button places the WordPerfect screen in a medium-sized frame within the larger Windows screen. Note that the Restore button changes to a Maximize button that appears as an up arrow.

Maximize button enlarges the WordPerfect screen to the full-screen size.

Button bar contains buttons that you can use instead of the pull-down menus to select specialized WordPerfect functions.

Vertical scroll bar enables you to scroll through pages of text in a document. The icons which resemble pages, and are located beneath the down arrow enable you to use the mouse to view the preceding page and the next page.

Ln. Identifies the vertical position of the insertion point, measured from the top edge of the page. By default, this measurement is shown in inches.

Pg. Indicates the number of the page on which the insertion point is located.

Pos. Identifies the horizontal position of the insertion point, measured from the left edge of the page, and also shown in inches.

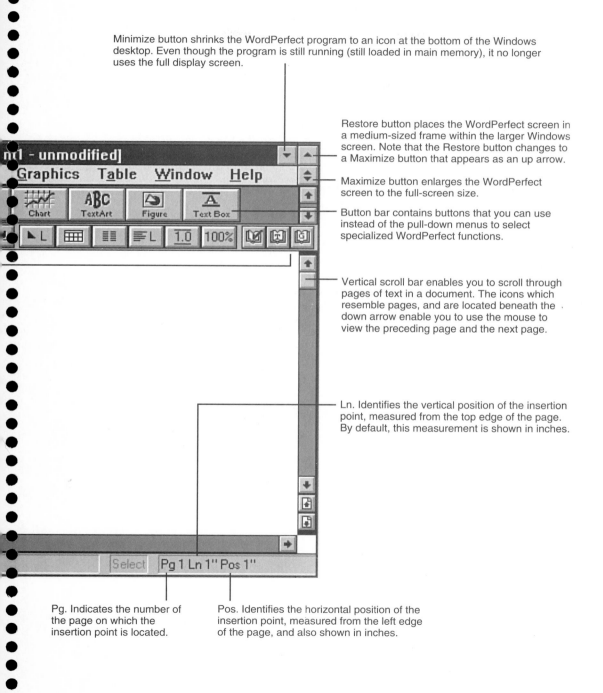

1.3: To Use the Mouse

You can use the mouse in the WordPerfect program to choose menu options or select elements in a document. You can also use the mouse to select document text as well as to select, move, and size document windows and graphics in the program.

WordPerfect for Windows supports both a two-button and a three-button mouse. Most WordPerfect functions are accessed by using the left mouse button, although the right mouse button is used to access *QuickMenus* in WordPerfect.

Mouse buttons are used in three basic ways:

- *Clicking.* Pressing and then immediately releasing the mouse button.
- *Double-clicking.* Pressing and releasing the mouse button twice in rapid succession.
- *Dragging.* Pressing and holding the mouse button as you move the mouse.

The WordPerfect pull-down menus are normally displayed in the Menu bar at the top of the WordPerfect program window. Each menu contains various options that appear as soon as you open the menu by choosing it from the Menu bar.

To choose a WordPerfect pull-down menu, position the mouse pointer on the menu name and click the left mouse button. The menu name is highlighted, and opens to display all of the available menu options (see fig. 1.3).

Fig. 1.3
The Draft option is displayed in the View menu.

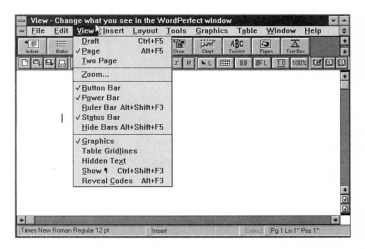

Exercise 2: Selecting Menu Commands with the Mouse

In this exercise you will open the View menu by using the mouse, and then choose a command from the pull-down menu.

1. Position the mouse pointer on View.

2. Click the left mouse button.

   WordPerfect displays a pull-down menu.

3. Click a command name to execute it.

   You are returned to the WordPerfect screen.

4. To cancel a pull-down menu, press ⟨Alt⟩ or click the menu's name.

NOTE If a menu command appears dimmed (a light gray), it is not currently available for selection. If a check mark precedes a command, the command can be toggled on and off. When key combinations follow an option, you can use that keyboard shortcut to select the command without accessing the pull-down menus. If a menu option is followed by an ellipsis (…), a dialog box with additional options appears as soon as you select the option. If an option is followed by a right-pointing triangle (▶), a cascading menu containing more options appears when you choose that option. After the cascading menu is displayed, you can choose any of its available options (see fig. 1.4).

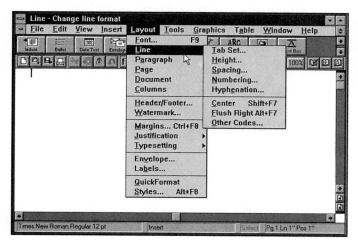

Fig. 1.4
Choosing the Line command on the Layout menu opens a cascading menu.

In addition to regular menus, a set of QuickMenus are included in the WordPerfect for Windows program. QuickMenus appear directly from on-screen objects such as the Power bar, Button bar, Status bar, and scroll bars.

Unit 1: Getting Started

To Select QuickMenu Commands with the mouse, follow these steps:

1. Position the mouse pointer anywhere on the Power Bar (refer to fig. 1.2 if you need help finding the Power bar).

2. Click the right mouse button to display the QuickMenu. WordPerfect displays a pull-down menu containing the Preferences and Hide Power Bar options.

3. To choose an option, point to the option and click the left mouse button.

When you choose the Preferences option from the File menu, you see a dialog box from which you can choose additional options. If you choose Hide Power Bar, you are returned to the WordPerfect screen, and the Power bar no longer is displayed.

Dialog Boxes

If a menu option is followed by an ellipsis (...), WordPerfect displays a dialog box containing additional options. Dialog boxes request additional information about a menu choice, and display warnings and program messages that inform you of the status of a command, or tell you why WordPerfect is unable to carry out a command.

To choose options from a dialog box, perform the following steps:

1. Open a menu option from the Menu bar, such as the File menu.

2. Select an option from the menu, such as Print.

   The Print dialog box appears providing additional options from which you can choose, such as the number of copies to be printed, the print quality, and the print color.

3. Choose Close, and you are returned to the WordPerfect screen.

Exercise 3: Making Selections from a Dialog Box

In this exercise you will open a menu and enter information into a dialog box.

1. From the Menu bar, select File.

2. From the File menu, select Document Summary. A dialog box like the one shown in figure 1.5 will appear. This dialog box enables you to record basic information about the document on which you are working.

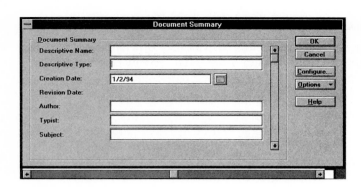

Fig. 1.5
Document
summary
dialog box.

3. Move the mouse pointer to the Descriptive Name: field and click once to anchor the insertion point. Type **Practice File**.

4. Press ⟨Tab⟩ to move to the next field, descriptive type. Type **Junk File**.

5. Press ⟨Tab⟩ again. Notice that the creation date has automatically been entered with the system date (which should be the correct date).

6. Move to the Author field and enter your name.

7. Complete any other fields that you wish to and then click on OK when you have finished.

1.4: To Learn the Keyboard

With WordPerfect for Windows, you use the following areas of the keyboard:

- The function keys are labeled F1 to F12 and are located at the top of an enhanced keyboard.

- The alphanumeric or "typing" keys are located in the center of the keyboard. This area includes special keys such as ⟨Esc⟩, ⟨Ctrl⟩, ⟨Alt⟩, ⟨⇧Shift⟩, ⟨⟵Backspace⟩, and ⟨↵Enter⟩.

- The numeric and cursor-movement keys are located on the right side of the keyboard.

Function Keys

In WordPerfect for Windows, you can choose many commands by using either pull-down menus or their function-key equivalents. WordPerfect assigns up to six functions to each function key, depending on whether the key is used alone or in combination with ⟨⇧Shift⟩, ⟨Alt⟩, ⟨Alt⟩+⟨⇧Shift⟩, ⟨Ctrl⟩, or ⟨Ctrl⟩+⟨⇧Shift⟩.

The Alphanumeric Keys

The alphanumeric keys are similar to those on a typewriter. In addition to the number, letter, and punctuation keys in the standard QWERTY arrangement, the alphanumeric keys include [Tab ↹], [Caps Lock], [← Backspace], [↵ Enter], [⇧ Shift], [Ctrl] (Control), and [Alt] (Alternate).

The function of [↵ Enter] on a computer keyboard is much different than that of a carriage return on a typewriter. [↵ Enter] is used to end a paragraph or a short line of text. You do not need to press [↵ Enter] at the end of a normal line that continues, the *word wrap* feature in WordPerfect automatically moves text to the next line for you, and keeps the text within the predefined margins.

Cursor-Movement Keys and the Numeric Keypad

The insertion point is the flashing vertical bar (referred to as a cursor) that marks the place in the document where the next character you type will appear. In addition, the cursor indicates where hidden formatting codes will be inserted (for example codes used to begin a new font style). In a WordPerfect document, you can use the direction keys on the cursor-movement keypad to move the insertion point through text. Note, however, that pressing one of these keys has no effect in places where you haven't yet entered text.

The numeric keypad contains both direction and numeric keys. To move the insertion point with these keys, you must turn off Num Lock. When Num Lock is turned on, WordPerfect enters numbers into your document instead of moving the insertion point. [Num Lock] is a toggle switch, which means that you press it once to turn it on and press it again to turn it off.

 STEPS

To open a pull-down menu and choose a command by using the keyboard, perform the following steps:

1. Press [Alt].

   Notice the dark highlight that appears on the menu bar.

2. Type the underlined letter of the name of the option you want to display. (In this book, the underlined letter on-screen is represented by boldfaced type.)

   WordPerfect displays the pull-down menu.

3. To choose a command from the pull-down menu, type the underlined letter of the command, or use the cursor-movement keys to highlight the command you want to execute, and then press [↵ Enter].

Exercise 4: Viewing the Document Summary Using the Keyboard

In this exercise you will review the document summary you created in Exercise 3 using the keyboard to access the menus instead of the mouse.

1. Press Alt to activate the keyboard menu.

2. Press **F** to pull down the File menu.

3. Press **Y** to access the Document Summary.

4. Review the document summary information.

5. Press the Tab⇥ key until the Cancel button is activated (a dotted box appears around the word cancel). Press ↵Enter.

1.5: To Exit WordPerfect for Windows

As with any other computer program, you must exit WordPerfect for Windows when you are finished working. When you exit a program properly, you ensure that the documents you have created are closed out of memory and safely stored on disk.

To exit WordPerfect using the mouse, follow these steps:

STEPS

1. Select the File menu.

2. Select Exit.

3. If you have entered information into the active document, WordPerfect will ask you to save the document. If no information has been entered, you will automatically be exited and returned to the Windows Program Manager.

Exercise 5: Exiting WordPerfect for Windows

In this exercise you will exit WordPerfect 6 for Windows.

1. Select the appropriate menu items to exit WordPerfect.

2. Because you entered information into the document summary, WordPerfect will ask if you wish to save the changes that you made to document1, as shown in figure 1.6.

Fig. 1.6
WordPerfect asks
if you wish to save
the changes that
you made to
Document1.

3. Since this file was just a practice file, you will not save the changes (thus, no document will be saved in this particular instance). Click **No**.

Unit Summary

In this unit, you learned how to start the WordPerfect for Windows program, and how to use the mouse and the keyboard. You also learned the various components of a WordPerfect for Windows screen.

New Terms

To test your knowledge of the new terms in this unit, consult the glossary at the end of this book.

- Icons
- Windows
- WordPerfect program window
- Insertion point
- Document window
- Click
- Double-click
- Drag
- Dialog box
- Cursor (insertion point)
- File name
- Hard return
- Soft return
- Word wrap
- Insert mode
- Typeover mode

Creating a Document

2

In this unit you learn how to create, save, and print a document. You learn the difference between using Typeover mode and Insert mode when entering text, and you learn how to use different views to examine a document.

2.1: To Start a New Document

When you start WordPerfect for Windows, the program displays a blank, full-size document window in which you can enter text for your new document. WordPerfect automatically assigns the temporary name Document1 to the first open document window until you use the **File Save** or **File Save As** command to name and save the file. This temporary name appears in the Title bar of the document window (see fig. 2.1).

Unit 2: Creating a Document

Fig. 2.1
A document
window displaying
the default docu-
ment name,
DOCUMENT1.

WordPerfect for Windows enables you to have as many as nine documents open at one time.

 STEPS

To open a new document in a separate WordPerfect window, perform the following steps:

1. Open the **File** menu.

2. Choose **New**.

Notice that the name on the Title bar is no longer Document1; the name is Document2 because Document2 is now the active document window. If you already have a document window open, such as Document1, WordPerfect for Windows assigns the next available numbered default name to your new document window, in this case Document2 (see fig. 2.2).

Fig. 2.2
The document
screen displaying
a new window,
Document2.

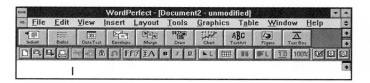

Although being able to create a new document is important, you will find that you need to edit an existing document more often. To edit a pre-viously written document, you must retrieve that document into a WordPerfect window.

 STEPS

To retrieve an existing document into the document window, perform the following steps:

1. Open the **File** menu.

2. Choose **Open**.

   WordPerfect displays the Open File dialog box (see fig 2.3).

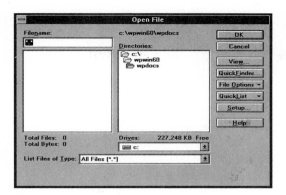

Fig. 2.3
The Open File
dialog box.

3. Highlight a file name from the desired file listing, and double-click the left mouse button; or type the name of the file you want to retrieve in the Filename text box, and press ↵Enter.

When you have finished working with a document, it is a good idea to close the document. To close a document you must select the **Close** option from the **File** menu. This option will close the active document (check the Title bar to make sure you're closing the right window!).

To close the active document, perform the following steps:

1. Open the **File** menu.

2. Choose **Close**.

Selecting a Template for a New Document

WordPerfect for Windows contains over 40 document templates. A *template* is a ready-made document that may contain text, formatting settings, view options (such as hiding or displaying the Button Bar and Power Bar), and graphic images. The supplied templates provide attractive and useful document designs that can save you a great deal of time. When you open a new document, WordPerfect for Windows automatically uses the standard template. Figure 2.4 shows that the standard template is selected in the Templates dialog box.

There may be times when you want to use a template other than the standard template. You can view and select different templates from the Templates dialog box.

Fig. 2.4
The Templates
dialog box.

 STEPS

To view a template, perform the following steps:

1. Open the File menu.

2. Choose Template.

   The Templates dialog box appears, with the standard option highlighted.

3. Click on the template you wish to see.

4. Click the View option button in the dialog box to preview the selected template.

   A smaller window appears (called the Viewer) displaying the selected template. Figure 2.5 shows a view of the resume template.

Fig. 2.5
The Viewer
window displaying
the resume
template.

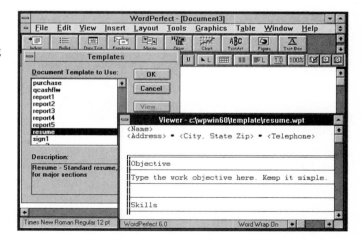

5. Double-click the Document Control button in the upper left corner of the Viewer window to return to the Template dialog box.

6. In the Templates dialog box, choose Cancel to return to the WordPerfect screen or choose OK to use the template.

Understanding WordPerfect's Default Settings

When you start WordPerfect, the program puts into effect a number of *default settings.* These default settings affect the way the program interacts with you, the way information is displayed, and the initial formatting used in each new document you create. Typically, the defaults include margin settings, line spacing, justification settings, and tab settings. You can change these default settings by using the **F**ile **P**references command, which is discussed in Unit 7.

Exercise 1: Beginning a Memo

In this exercise you will start WordPerfect, open a new document, and select a template for a memo-style letter. You will enter the text for this memo in the next exercise.

1. Start WordPerfect. Refer back to Unit 1 if you need help.

2. With a blank document facing you, make menu selections to use a template.

3. From the Templates dialog box, select the memo5 template and click on OK.

4. WordPerfect has an *autofill macro* feature that allows you to fill in information in a dialog box once, and then the program uses that information anytime you start a template-type document. If you are working on your own computer, feel free to enter your information into the Autofill Macro dialog box. If, however, you are working on a computer used by many different people, click Cancel when the dialog box comes up.

5. The memo5 template should be displayed on your screen, as shown in figure 2.6.

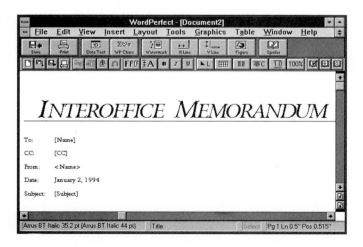

Fig. 2.6
The memo5 template is displayed as Document2.

2.2: To Enter Text

To begin entering text in a new document, simply start typing. As you type, characters appear at the location of the cursor (insertion point) and the number represented by the POS indicator in the status bar increases. Unlike typewritten or handwritten methods, word processors enable you to make major revisions in seconds. You can delete, move, format, or copy entire pages of text with one or two keystrokes.

Understanding the Insertion Point

The flashing vertical bar in the WordPerfect screen text area is the insertion point. When you open a new document, the insertion point appears in the upper left corner. The insertion point moves to the right as text is inserted and shows you where you are in a document. You can move the insertion point through existing text by using the cursor-movement keys or the mouse. You cannot move the insertion point through a blank text area.

Understanding the Word Wrap Feature

When using a typewriter, you must always be aware of when you will reach the end of a line so that you can insert a carriage return. WordPerfect's *word wrap* feature keeps track of the insertion point as it moves toward the right margin, and when the text has filled a line, word wrap automatically drops text to the next line. With word wrap, you need to press ⏎Enter only when you want to begin a new paragraph or create extra spacing. Each time the word wrap feature drops text down to a new line, a [SRt] (soft return) code is inserted into the document. Each time you press ⏎Enter, an [HRt] code (hard return) is inserted. You can see these hidden codes when you view the Reveal Codes window (see fig 2.7).

Fig. 2.7
The [HRt] and [SRt] codes are displayed in the Reveal Codes window.

Document window —

Hard return code —
Soft return codes —

Reveal Codes window —

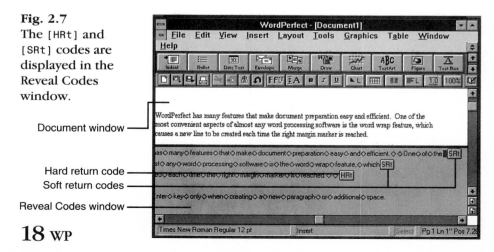

Exercise 2: Using Word Wrap

To see how the word wrap feature works, type the paragraph exactly as shown in figure 2.8 (including spelling and grammatical errors) in the memo5 template that you retrieved in Exercise 1. Press ⏎Enter twice after the last period of each paragraph. This memo will be used in subsequent exercises.

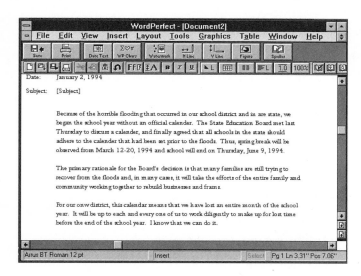

Fig. 2.8
Type the text shown in this window.

Moving through Text with the Mouse

The quickest way to reposition the cursor in existing text is by using the mouse. Simply position the I-beam pointer so that it is between the characters in the text that need editing, and click the left mouse button.

Moving through Text with the Keyboard

WordPerfect offers various key combinations that you can use to move through text using the keyboard, many of which not only move the cursor in the text, but also scroll the document. Sometimes it's faster to use keyboard combination methods than it is to use the vertical scroll bar and the mouse. Table 2.1 shows key combinations used to move through a document.

Table 2.1	Moving the Cursor through Text with the Keyboard
Key(s)	*Cursor Movement in Text*
↑	Moves up one line
↓	Moves down one line
←	Moves one position to the left
→	Moves one position to the right
Ctrl + →	Moves to the beginning of the next word to the right
Ctrl + ←	Moves to the beginning of the next word to the left
Ctrl + ↑	Moves up one paragraph
Ctrl + ↓	Moves down one paragraph
PgUp	Moves to the top of the active document window
PgDn	Moves to the bottom of the active document window
Home	Moves to the beginning of the line
End	Moves to the end of the line
Alt + Home	Moves to the beginning of the page
Alt + End	Moves to the end of the page
Ctrl + Home	Moves to the beginning of the document
Ctrl + End	Moves to the end of the document

Exercise 3: Using Key Combinations to Move through a Document

In this exercise you will practice moving around in the memo that you wrote in Exercise 2.

1. Move to the top of the document by pressing Home + Home + ↑.

2. Move to the bottom of the document by pressing Home + Home + ↓.

3. Place the cursor at the beginning of the second paragraph using the mouse pointer.

4. Move the cursor right one word by using Ctrl+→.

5. Practice using other navigation options discussed in table 2.1.

Understanding Insert Mode

As you type text in a new document, WordPerfect uses the default setting of *Insert mode*, which inserts the text to the left of the insertion point, moving the existing text to the right. You toggle Insert mode on and off by pressing Ins. When you are using Insert mode, the word Insert appears in the Status bar.

When you want to replace existing text with new text, you can use *Typeover mode*, which replaces existing characters or spaces with the new characters you type at the cursor's position. Typeover mode is the alternative mode to Insert and is activated by pressing Ins.

Exercise 4: Replacing Text with Typeover Mode

In this exercise you will fill in the top of the memo form using Typeover mode to overwrite the printed information.

1. Position the cursor to the left of the text: [Name].

2. Press the Ins key once to change from insert to Typeover mode. Check the status line at the bottom of the screen to make sure it says Typeover.

3. Type **All faculty, staff, and students**.

4. Move the cursor down to the CC: line to the left of [CC].

5. Type **Green County School Board**.

6. Move the cursor to the From line, to the left of <Name> and type **Jayne Evans, Principal**.

7. The date should already be filled in.

8. On the subject line, anchor the cursor to the left of [Subject] and type **New school calender**.

9. Press the Ins key once again to return to Insert mode.

Using Backspace and Delete

You can use ⌫Backspace and Del to correct errors as you type a document. Pressing ⌫Backspace deletes the character to the left of the cursor, and pressing Del deletes the character to the right of the cursor. To edit previously typed text, you can use the arrow keys with ⌫Backspace and Del to navigate through the document and make corrections.

⚠ WARNING
Both ⌫Backspace and Del are repeating keys, which means that if you press and hold down either of these keys, WordPerfect will continue to delete characters until you release the key.

 STEPS

To use Del to correct an error in the document, perform the following steps:

1. Using the appropriate arrow keys, move the cursor to the left of the letter you wish to delete.

2. Press the Del key.

3. The letter is deleted, and the remaining text moves to the left.

STEPS

Follow these steps to use ⌫Backspace to correct a mistake:

1. Use the arrow keys to move the cursor to the right of the letter you wish to delete.

2. Press ⌫Backspace to delete the character.

Exercise 5: Correcting Errors in the Memo

In this exercise you will correct two errors in the memo.

1. Use the Del key method to delete the *y* in Jayne Evans' first name.

2. Use the ⌫Backspace key method to delete the word *are* in the first sentence of the first paragraph.

3. Enter **our** as replacement text for the word *are* that you just deleted.

4. Leave the document on screen for now. You'll correct the remaining errors in subsequent exercises.

2.3: To View a Document

As you type text, it is displayed in *Page mode*, which is the default setting for WordPerfect. Page mode displays headers and footers and enables you to view the font you are using.

An alternative option, *Draft mode*, offers you the same *WYSIWYG* features but enables the screen display to react more quickly as you type and scroll through text. Headers and footers are not shown in Draft mode. You may find Draft mode more suitable when you are entering text into the document, and then later you can return to Page mode to see how the document actually appears.

To change from Page mode to Draft mode, perform the following steps:

STEPS

1. Open the View menu.

2. Choose the Draft option.

When the document screen reappears, the repositioned cursor is displayed, and the space for the header and footer has been removed.

If you want to see where the tabs, spaces, and ends of paragraphs occur in the document, you can view these formatting symbols by choosing the Show option from the View menu.

To view the formatting symbols in the current document, perform the following steps:

STEPS

1. Open the View menu.

2. Choose the Show option.

Your document screen displays the formatting symbols (see fig. 2.9).

Fig. 2.9
The document screen with the Show Option feature activated.

STEPS To remove formatting symbols from the document window, perform the following steps:

1. Open the View menu.

2. Choose the Show option again to remove the check mark and deactivate the symbol display.

Using the Zoom Option

You can enlarge or reduce the view of text or graphics on-screen with View Zoom to see more on-screen information at one time. By magnifying the view, you can examine images and text in detail.

 STEPS To use the Zoom option, perform the following steps:

1. Open the View menu.

2. Choose Zoom.

   WordPerfect displays the Zoom dialog box, showing various percentage option buttons used to magnify or reduce the screen display.

3. Choose a percentage option button.

4. Choose the OK button.

   Your screen display shows the enlargement or reduction.

5. Return your display to 100% when finished.

2.4: To Save a Document

After you create a document, you can save it for later retrieval. Because the displayed document is temporary (until you save the document to disk), the contents of the document are lost when you turn off the machine. The following section shows you how to save a document the first time, and then resave existing documents.

File names for documents can contain up to eight characters and include an optional extension of up to three characters. Spaces are not allowed in a file name.

 STEPS To save the document the first time, perform the following steps:

1. Open the File menu.

2. Choose Save As.

The Save As dialog box appears with an insertion point flashing in the Filename box.

3. Type a valid file name in the Filename box.

4. Choose OK to complete the Save As procedure.

Saving an Existing Document

After saving a document the first time, you can save it again by choosing the Save option from the File menu. WordPerfect saves the document for you without your having to issue additional commands because the program defaults to the file name used the first time you saved the document.

To save a document with the same file name, follow these steps:

1. Select File from the menu.

2. Select Save.

Sometimes you will want to save a previously saved document under a different file name. This is especially true when you want to make a backup copy before making major editing changes. After you have saved your document with a file name, you can save a copy of it under a new name by accessing the File menu and choosing the Save As option. This procedure opens the Save As dialog box, in which you can edit the file name and change the directory and/ or drive.

Exercise 6: Saving the Memo file

In this exercise you will save the memo file you wrote in this unit using the Save As command.

1. From the File menu, select Document Summary and fill in the document summary page with information about yourself.

2. Using Save As, save the memo file with the file name **calendar.mem** onto your floppy (A:) disk.

2.5: To Print a Document

To print a hard copy of the document using WordPerfect's default print settings, perform the following steps:

1. Open the File menu.

2. Choose **P**rint. The Print dialog box appears.

3. Choose the **P**rint option button.

   The message Preparing Document for Printing appears to inform you that the file is being readied for printing.

   The default print settings that are used include

   - Printing the full document
   - Using the selected printer
   - Printing one copy

Exercise 7: Printing the Calendar.mem file

For this exercise, print the file Calendar.mem that you worked on in this unit. Use the default printer settings unless your instructor asks you to do something different. Exit WordPerfect, saving the document again when WordPerfect prompts.

Unit Summary

In this unit you created and entered text into a new document and then edited that document. You learned how to use the different viewing options, how to save a document, and how to print a hard copy of a document.

New Terms

To check your knowledge of the new terms in this unit, consult the glossary at the end of this book.

- Template
- Default setting
- Word wrap
- Page mode
- Draft mode
- WYSIWYG
- Autofill macro

Editing Your Documents

In this unit, you learn to work with multiple documents. You learn to select text for copying, cutting, and pasting; and you also learn to use the WordPerfect Help feature.

3.1: To Open Existing Documents for Editing

Before you can edit the contents of a WordPerfect for Windows document you have saved to disk, you must open the document into a document window.

 STEPS To open an existing document, perform the following steps:

1. Start WordPerfect for Windows using one of the methods described in Unit 1.

2. Open the **File** menu; then choose **Open**. WordPerfect displays the Open File dialog box listing all of the files in the current directory.

3. Click once on the name of the document you want to open and press ⏎Enter.

You also can double-click the name of the file to open it. If you get a message saying that the file is not found, check to make sure that the drive and directory are correct.

The Open File dialog box includes the following options not yet discussed:

- *QuickFinder.* Use QuickFinder to search for specific files according to their file pattern, words or phrases, summary fields, date ranges, or the QuickFinder Index.

- *List Files of Type box.* Click the arrow next to this box to activate a drop-down list which contains options that enable you to choose the type of files you want to display in the Files list box.

- *View.* Use View to see a file before opening it into the document window.

Opening a Document from a Different Drive or Directory

You may need to access a file from a drive or directory other than the default drive or directory. If you are using a hard drive (usually drive C), WordPerfect considers this drive to be the default. During the installation of the program, WordPerfect sets up one directory to store its program files (\WPWIN60), and a separate directory to store your work files (WPDOCS). When attempting to access information from a drive other than the drive C, you need to specify where you want WordPerfect to look for the information.

 To open a file from the drive A, for example, follow these steps:

1. Be sure there is a disk in the drive you wish to access.

2. Open the File menu, and choose Open. The Open File dialog box appears.

3. Click the arrow next to the Drives box to activate the drop-down list containing the drives available to your computer.

4. Choose drive A. The file list and directory box show information on files and directories located in the drive A (see fig. 3.1).

Viewing the Contents of a Document

As the list of documents you create in WordPerfect grows, you may not be able to tell what information each file contains just by looking at the file name. You can use WordPerfect's File Viewer to quickly view a document's contents.

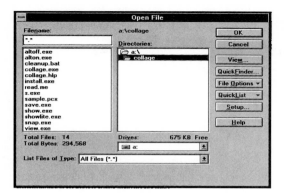

Fig. 3.1
The Open File
dialog box shows
a file list for
drive A.

When you choose the View command button within the Open File dialog box, WordPerfect opens a separate View window that enables you to look at the text of a chosen file. You can move through the text by using the scroll bars.

To view the contents of an existing file, perform the following steps: STEPS

1. Open the File menu; then choose Open.

   The Open File dialog box appears.

2. Click the file name of the document you wish to view to highlight it.

3. Click the View option in the dialog box. The Viewer window appears displaying the contents of the selected file, as shown in figure 3.2. You can maximize or scroll through this window.

4. To close the Viewer window, double-click the control button in the upper left corner of the Viewer window.

   WordPerfect returns you to the Open File dialog box.

5. Choose Cancel to return to the document window.

Exercise 1: Viewing the Calendar.mem file

In this exercise you will view the contents of the Calendar.mem file without actually retrieving the file for editing.

1. Insert your work disk from Unit 2 into the A: drive of your computer.

2. Start WordPerfect, if necessary.

3. Select the appropriate menu items to view A:Calendar.mem.

4. Notice the options you have in the Viewer window.

5. Close the Viewer window.

Fig. 3.2
The file you edited in Unit 2, Exercise 5 is shown in the Viewer window.

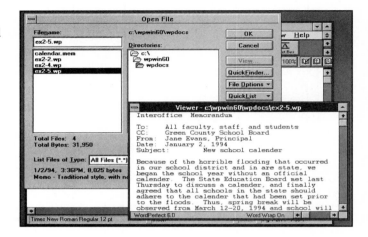

3.2: To Work with Multiple Documents

If your computer has sufficient memory, you can open as many as nine documents at one time in WordPerfect. Having multiple documents open makes it easy to transfer text from one document to another—a process generally called copy and paste.

 STEPS To open multiple documents in the WordPerfect document screen, perform the following steps:

1. Open the File menu; then choose Open.

   The Open File dialog box appears.

2. Hold down the [⇧Shift] key and click each file you want to open.

3. When all desired files are selected, choose OK.

   The document screen appears and briefly displays the contents of each file that you chose. Only the last open document window is visible in the WordPerfect window.

 TIP When you want a group of files opened that are adjacent to one another, you can drag the mouse across them to highlight them all at once, and then choose OK to open all selected files.

Viewing More than One Document Window

Each WordPerfect document you open appears in its own full-size document window. Each document window can be controlled with its own Maximize and Minimize buttons, drop-down menu, and scroll bars. To view more than one open document, you can resize and rearrange document windows using the Cascade or Tile options.

To arrange the open documents by using the Cascade option, perform the following step:

1. Open the Window menu; then choose Cascade.

    The windows of the opened files overlap one another. The active file window is displayed in front of all other windows, with its Title bar highlighted (see fig. 3.3).

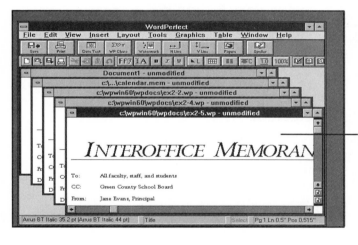

Fig. 3.3
The cascaded windows displaying ex2-5.wp as the active file.

— Active document window

To arrange documents by using the Tile option, do the following:

1. Open the Window menu, and choose Tile.

    The open files are displayed one above the other (see fig. 3.4). The Title bar of the active document is highlighted.

2. Once multiple files show in cascaded or tiled document windows, you must know how to activate the desired document for editing. For cascaded documents, simply click on the Title bar of the document you wish to edit. This will bring that document to the front of the stack. From there you can maximize the document's window and restore it when you have finished.

Fig. 3.4
The open documents in a tiled display.

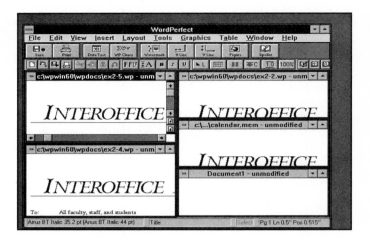

3. For tiled documents, click on the maximize button of the document you wish to edit. This will bring a full-size document window up. Restore the document when finished and you will be returned to the tiled view.

Closing Existing Document Windows

After you have finished with a document, you can close its window to free computer memory and reduce clutter on your screen. Before you can close a document window, you must make the document the active window (the window in which any changes or cursor movements will be made).

STEPS

To close the open documents currently on your screen, perform the following steps:

1. Click the Title bar for the document you wish to close to make it the active window.

2. Open the File menu; then choose Close.

3. Close all the remaining windows.

If you have made changes to the document in the window you are closing, WordPerfect prompts you to confirm your changes. To save changes before closing the window, choose the **Yes** button. To clear the active document window of text without closing the active window, press the Clear key combination, Ctrl + ⇧Shift + F4.

Retrieving One File into Another File

Sometimes you may want to incorporate the text of one document into the document in which you're working. WordPerfect makes this an easy task to perform.

To incorporate the text of one document into another document, perform the following steps:

STEPS

1. Retrieve the main document. This will be the document into which you insert the second file.

2. Anchor the I-beam where you want the new text to be displayed.

3. Open the Insert menu; then choose File.

   The Insert File dialog box is displayed.

4. From the Insert file list, choose the document you wish to insert.

5. Choose Insert.

   WordPerfect displays a message asking you to confirm the insertion of the selected document into the current document.

6. Choose Yes.

7. The screen shows the edited document with the inserted text.

Exercise 2: Inserting One Document into Another

For this exercise, you will create a short memo to the School Board explaining the memo you plan to send to all teachers and students in your school regarding the calendar changes. You will then insert the Calendar.mem document into this memo. Be sure you have the disk on which you saved the Calendar.mem file from the last unit in drive A:.

1. Close any files that are open on your computer.

2. Open a new file and use the Letter5 template.

3. Edit the template so that your letter looks like the one in figure 3.5.

4. Save the document as **Board1-9.LTR** (the 1-9 indicates the date on which the letter was written).

5. Move the cursor to below the closing of the letter and press Ctrl + ⏎Enter to make a hard page break. The letter style automatically creates a second page with a heading. Don't worry about that for now.

Fig. 3.5
The new memo to
the school board.

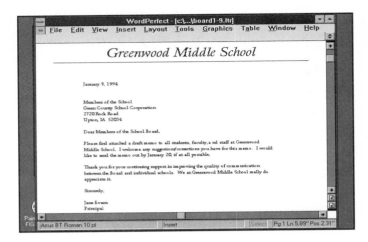

6. Insert the Calendar.mem, using the steps described above. Page 2 of the letter to the board should now contain the Calendar.mem text and format.

7. Save the document again and close the document.

3.3: To Select Text

WordPerfect enables you to perform a series of actions on a selected block of text without repeating the selection process. The following sections explain the procedure for selecting text using the keyboard and mouse and for making changes to selected text.

Using the Mouse To Select Text

In a WordPerfect document, you must select the text you want to modify before you can choose an editing command. WordPerfect displays the text you select by highlighting it, that is, showing the text in inverse video.

When you move the mouse pointer over text, the pointer changes from an arrowhead to an I-beam.

STEPS To select text using the mouse, follow these steps:

1. Position the I-beam immediately preceding the first character you want to select.

2. Drag the mouse to the right (to select words on a single line) and/or down (to select text on multiple lines) until all of the desired text is highlighted.

3. Release the mouse button. The text is highlighted.

4. To cancel the selection of the text, position the pointer anywhere outside the selected text and click again.

Using Shortcuts for Selecting Text

When selecting text with a mouse, you can use shortcuts that don't involve dragging. These shortcuts are as follows:

- To select a single word, double-click anywhere in the word.
- To select a sentence, triple-click (three rapid clicks in a row) anywhere in the sentence.
- To select a paragraph, quadruple-click (four rapid clicks in a row) anywhere in the paragraph.

Using QuickMenus To Select Text

You also can use the mouse to select a sentence, paragraph, or all text in a document without having to click or drag through the text. Instead you use the QuickMenu attached to the left margin of the document.

To open the QuickMenu and select text, perform the following steps:

1. Position the mouse pointer to the left of the text you wish to select.

2. Click the right mouse button.

    The QuickMenu appears (see fig. 3.6).

Fig. 3.6
The QuickMenu.

3. Choose Sentence to select the sentence on the current line. The sentence is highlighted.

You also can choose **Paragraph** to select the current paragraph, or **All** to select all the text in the document.

4. To cancel the selection, position the pointer in the right margin and click again.

Replacing Selected Text

You can replace a section of text by selecting the text you want to replace and then typing the replacement text. As soon as you type your first replacement character, WordPerfect deletes all of the selected text.

 STEPS

To replace the first sentence in the second paragraph with a new sentence, perform the following steps:

1. Drag the mouse over the desired text to select it.

2. Type the replacement text. The old text is removed, and the new text is inserted.

Inserting Blank Lines and Deleting Text

Press ⏎Enter to indicate the end of a paragraph and to insert blank lines in the text of your document. Pressing ⏎Enter inserts a blank line regardless of whether you are in Insert or Typeover mode.

To delete a block of text, use the mouse to select (highlight) the text you want to erase, and then press either ←Backspace or Del.

Using the Undo Command

You can use the Undo command to restore deleted text and to recover from other editing mistakes, such as choosing the wrong WordPerfect command. WordPerfect holds in memory the last action you made in the document and can restore the document to the state it was in before your last action. Remember that in order to reverse the last command you invoked, you must choose the Undo command before choosing another WordPerfect command.

Using the Undelete Command

Unlike the Undo command, which restores only the last deletion to a document, the Undelete command can restore any of the last three deletions.

To activate the Undelete command, follow these steps:

STEPS

1. Open the Edit menu; then choose Undelete.

   WordPerfect displays the Undelete dialog box (see fig. 3.7).

Fig. 3.7
The Undelete
dialog box.

2. Use the **Restore** button to restore the highlighted text, or the **Previous** button to restore the next-to-last deletion you made. You can continue to choose the **Next** or **Previous** button to cycle forward or backward through the last three deletions you made. When the text you want restored is displayed, choose the **Restore** button again to have the restorations take effect.

Exercise 3: Selecting, Deleting, and Restoring Text

In this exercise you will work on the Board1-9.ltr document.

1. Retrieve the Board1-9.ltr document if it is not already on your screen.

2. Select the last sentence in the first paragraph of the letter *I would like...*.

3. Replace the selected sentence with the following sentence: **Please have any changes to the memo back to me no later than January 17th, so that I may send the memo out on the 20th.**

4. Move to the last sentence in the second paragraph of the letter.

5. Select the word *really* and delete it.

6. Undelete the word *really*.

7. Save the document.

3.4: To Use the Copy, Cut, and Paste Commands

WordPerfect's Copy, Cut, and Paste commands (located on the Edit menu) enable you easily to move or copy blocks of text to new places in the same document or to other open documents. WordPerfect performs the cut, copy, and paste operations through the Clipboard, a storage place in RAM.

Moving Text

To move text from one area to another in a document, use the Cut and **Paste** commands. With this command sequence you will select the text to be moved, cut the text, position the cursor in the new location, and paste the text into that location.

 STEPS   To move text with Cut and Paste, follow these steps:

1. Select the text to be moved, using a selection method previously discussed.

2. Open the Edit menu; then choose Cut.

3. Position the cursor where you want the text to be moved.

4. Open the Edit menu; then choose **Paste**.

Using the Copy Command

Unlike the Cut command, which removes the selected text, the Copy command duplicates the selected text, which then can be placed either in the same document or another open document.

 STEPS   To copy text, follow these steps:

1. Select the text to be copied.

2. Open the Edit menu; then choose Copy.

3. Position the cursor at the place where you want the text to be copied. Note that this can be in the same document or in a different document.

4. Open the Edit menu; then choose **Paste**.

Exercise 4: Using Cut, Copy, and Paste

In this exercise you will edit the Calendar.mem document using cut and paste to move some text.

1. Open the Calendar.mem document if it is not already opened.

2. Cut the first sentence in the last paragraph and paste it after the last sentence in the first paragraph.

3. Save the document.

4. Repeat step 2 in the Board1-9.ltr document.

5. Save the changes to the Board1-9.ltr document.

3.5: To Use WordPerfect Help

WordPerfect for Windows offers extensive on-line help in a special Help window, which you can access at any time while using the program. You can display the Help window along with your document by resizing and rearranging both windows.

Most Help topics contain cross-references, indicated by an underlined keyword or phrase in the Help text. On a color monitor the keyword or phrase is displayed in green as well as being underlined. Each cross-reference leads to related Help topics that give you additional information.

To select a cross-reference and display a related Help topic using the mouse, perform the following steps: STEPS

1. Open the Help menu, and choose Contents.

   Topics that appear in green on a color monitor include additional sub-topic information.

2. Position the mouse pointer on the WordPerfect Bars option. Notice that the pointer changes into a hand with a pointing finger (see fig. 3.8).

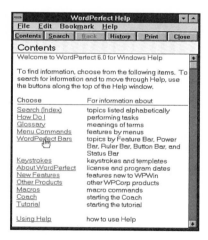

Fig. 3.8
Choosing a topic from the Contents menu of the Help command.

3. Click the topic WordPerfect Bars.

   A new Help window appears with subtopics of information for the different WordPerfect bars.

4. Click the topic Button Bar to see specific information for the Button Bar.

Using the Help Command Buttons

The Help window contains five command buttons, which you can use to navigate through Help topics. These buttons include:

- *Contents.* Activates the WordPerfect Help Contents command.
- *Search.* Enables you to search for specific Help topics that contain keywords.
- *Back.* Displays the most recent Help topic you selected and moves you back through topics you have selected.
- *History.* Displays the History dialog box, which lists previously viewed topics.
- *Print.* Prints the current Help topic.

Getting Context-Sensitive Help

WordPerfect supplies context-sensitive help that is directly related to the action you are performing. You can access context-sensitive help while in a dialog box, menu, or window.

 STEPS

To get context-sensitive help about a particular button on the WordPerfect Button Bar, perform the following steps:

1. Position the cursor on the Button Bar for Draw.
2. Press ⇧Shift+F1.

   A question mark inside of a bubble appears next to the pointer.
3. With the pointer and the bubble positioned on the Draw button, click once.

   WordPerfect displays the Help window for the Draw button.
4. Choose Close to return to the document.

Using the Coaches

The Coach command in WordPerfect for Windows gives you step-by-step instructions for performing common tasks.

 STEPS

To use the coach feature, perform the following steps:

1. Open the Help menu, and choose Coach.

   The Coach dialog box appears (see fig. 3.9).

Fig. 3.9
The Coach
dialog box.

2. Select the desired task from the list box; then choose OK.

    Instructions from WordPerfect Coach appear on-screen.

3. Choose the Continue button to walk through the steps.

    When the Coach instructs you to do something, you can either per-
    form the action or choose the Show Me button, which shows you the
    action to be performed. Use the Hint button to get more information
    about a step.

Exercise 5: Learning from the Coach

In this exercise you will get coaching help on creating a bulleted list.

1. Select the appropriate menu options to get the Coach dialog box on
    screen.

2. From the dialog box, select Bullets and click on OK.

3. Using coaching help, create the recipe shown in figure 3.10.

```
Easy Dill Dip
Mix the following ingredients, chill, and serve with fresh veggies or bread.

    ›    2 Cups Sour Cream
    ›    2 Cups Mayonaise
    ›    4 teaspoons Dill Seed
    ›    4 teaspoons Bon Appetit
    ›    4 Tablespoons Minced Onion Flakes
    ›    4 Tablespoons Parsley Flakes
```

Fig. 3.10
Use Coaching
to create a
bulleted list.

4. Save the recipe as: **DILLDIP.RCP**.

Unit Summary

In this unit, you learned how to open and close existing documents, how to cut, copy, and paste, and how to use the WordPerfect Help windows.

New Terms

To test your knowledge of the new terms in this unit, consult the glossary at the end of this book.

- Clipboard
- Select
- Cut
- Copy
- Paste

Proofreading Your Documents

In this unit, you learn how to use the Reveal Codes window to view hidden codes, and how to locate and replace text by using the Find and Replace feature. You also learn how to use the Speller, Thesaurus, and the Grammatik tools. No matter how carefully you enter and edit text, it can usually benefit from proofreading to correct misspellings and weak grammar.

4.1: To Work with Hidden Codes

As you learned in Unit 1, WordPerfect inserts hidden codes into the text of your document as you use various commands. These codes control how your document is formatted when printed. When you open the Reveal Codes window, you can edit the text or the codes in a document.

Deleting Hidden Codes

Deleting codes in the Reveal Codes window is usually more efficient than deleting codes from the editing

Objectives

When you have finished this unit you will have learned the following:

4.1 To Work with Hidden Codes

4.2 To Use the Find and Replace Features

4.3 To Use the Spell Checker

4.4 To Use the Thesaurus

4.5 To Use the Grammar Checker

screen because in the Reveal Codes window you can more easily identify the location of the codes within the document. Note that as you delete codes in the Reveal Codes window, the editing window reflects your changes.

STEPS

To delete a hidden code in the Reveal Codes window, follow these steps:

1. Open the document you want to edit.

2. Open the **View** menu; then choose **R**eveal Codes.

3. Position the cursor before the hidden code you want to delete.

   In figure 4.1, the cursor is positioned before the [Left Tab] code in the Reveal Codes window.

Fig. 4.1
The cursor is positioned in the Reveal Codes window.

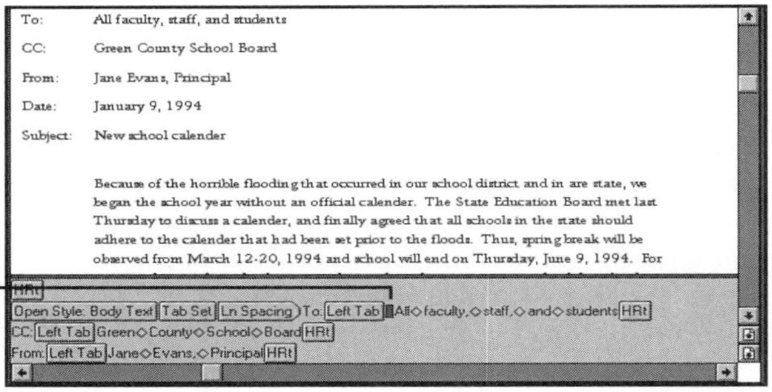

Cursor ——————

4. Press (Del).

   Note that the text in the editing window reflects any changes made in the Reveal Codes window. In this example, the deletion of the [Left Tab] code forces the text to align with the left margin.

5. Open the **View** menu, and choose **R**eveal Codes again to turn off the Reveal Codes feature.

   NOTE It is easy to delete a hidden code accidentally. If this happens, remember to use the **U**ndo command right away to restore the hidden code.

4.2: To Use the Find and Replace Features

The Find feature enables you to search for a character, a word, a phrase, or a hidden code either before or after the cursor's position. The set of characters (or characters and codes) that you want to locate in the document is called a *string*. The Find feature enables you to quickly locate sections of a document that require editing.

You can direct WordPerfect to search the entire document from the beginning or from the insertion point location to the end of the document. By choosing the Wrap at Beg./End of Document option, you can instruct WordPerfect to continue the search until it reaches the insertion point again. In order to find all occurrences of a string without regard to capitalization, you must type the string in all lowercase letters.

To locate all occurrences of a word in a document, perform the following steps:

1. Move the cursor to the top of the document to begin the search.

2. Open the Edit menu, and choose Find.

   WordPerfect displays the Find Text dialog box, shown in figure 4.2.

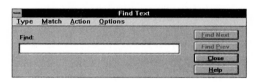

Figure 4.2
The Find Text dialog box enables you to enter information to search for in a document.

3. Type the text you wish to search for into the Find text box, and press ⏎Enter).

   WordPerfect highlights the first occurrence of the word.

4. To search the remainder of the document for additional occurrences of the desired word, choose the Find Next button.

5. Continue to choose Find Next until WordPerfect prompts you with a message box displaying a message saying that the word is not found. This message box indicates that no additional occurrences have been located.

6. Choose OK.

7. To search back through the text, choose the Find Previous button in the Find Text dialog box.

8. Select Close to close the dialog box.

Using Options with the Find Command

The following search options are available in the Find Text dialog box.

Choose **Type** to select the following option:

- *Specific Codes*. Use this option to search for a specific hidden code, such as [SRt] or [Right Tab]. The dialog box for this option supplies a list from which you can choose the codes you want to locate.

Choose **Match** to select from the following options:

- **W**hole Word. Use this option to avoid finding words that contain the search string. For example, when searching for the word *farm*, WordPerfect finds all words in the document containing the word *farm*, such as *farmer*, *farming*, and *farmed*. The **W**hole Word option is an alternative to typing a space before or after the word for which you are searching.

- *Case*. Use this option to locate words or phrases that exactly match the case of the search string; for example, you might want to search for *dBASE* but not *dBase*.

- *Font*. Use this option to locate text typed in a specific font and font size.

- *Codes*. Use this option to locate formatting codes.

Choose **Action** to select from the following options:

- *Select Match*. Use this option, and WordPerfect automatically selects the search string when it finds it in the text. This option is the default.

- *Position Before*. Use this option to have WordPerfect automatically select the search string and place the cursor before the located text.

- *Position After*. Use this option to have WordPerfect automatically select the search string and place the cursor after the located text.

- *Extend Selection*. Use this option when you select text before initiating a search to make WordPerfect extend the selection of text up to and including the text for which you have searched.

Choose **Options** to select from the following options:

- *Begin Find at Top of Document*. Use this option to search the entire document from the top.

- *Wrap at Beg./End of Document*. Use this option to search from the cursor forward and then from the top of the document to the insertion point.

- *Limit Find Within Selection*. Use this option when you select text before opening the Find text dialog box in order to limit the search to the selected text.

- *Include Headers, Footers, Etc.* Use this option to speed the search process by excluding the searching of such elements as headers, footers, footnotes, and endnotes.

Using Wild-Card Characters To Search for Text

WordPerfect includes two *wild-card characters* that you can use in a search string when you are uncertain of the spelling of a particular word or phrase in the document. The ? (question mark) replaces one character, and the * (asterisk) replaces several characters.

To use a wild-card character to search a document for unknown characters, perform the following steps:

STEPS

1. To begin your search, position the cursor at the top of the document that you created earlier in this unit.

2. Open the Edit menu; then choose Find.

3. In the Find text box, type the portion of the text you wish to search for (the letters of which you are sure).

4. Open the Match menu.

5. Choose Codes to open the Codes dialog box.

6. Scroll through the Find Codes list box until *(Many Char) is high-lighted, and double-click it. (It is the first option at the top of the list, see fig. 4.3). Or, if you are unsure of only one character, select ? (One Char).

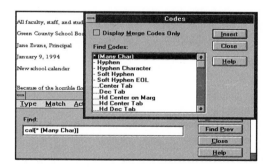

Fig. 4.3
The *(Many Char) option is selected from the Codes dialog box.

7. Choose Close.

   The [*(Many Char)] code is inserted into the Find text box after the word *brain* (see fig. 4.3).

8. Choose the Find Next button.

   WordPerfect begins the search and highlights the first occurrence of the search string.

Using the Replace Feature

The Replace feature is similar to the Find feature; however, when you use Replace, you enter a replacement string as well as a search string. You can use the Replace feature to replace a string of text or codes with different text or codes, or to remove the string completely from the document.

 STEPS

To replace an existing word with a new word, perform the following steps:

1. Position the cursor at the top of the document.

2. Open the **Edit** menu; then choose **R**eplace.

   WordPerfect displays the Find and Replace Text dialog box.

3. Type the word to be replaced into the **F**ind text box.

4. Type the replacement word in the Replace **W**ith box (see figure 4.4).

    NOTE Enter text for the replacement string exactly as you want it to appear. Include any capitalization and punctuation that is to be entered. If you want to remove text or codes from the document using the Replace feature, leave the Replace **W**ith text box blank.

Fig. 4.4
The Find and
Replace Text
dialog box.

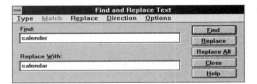

5. Choose **R**eplace.

   WordPerfect highlights the first occurrence of the search string.

6. Choose **R**eplace again to replace the old text with the new text.

7. Continue choosing **R**eplace until the message `Next Not Found` appears. This message indicates that WordPerfect has located the last occurrence of the search string. Select OK.

8. Choose **C**lose to return to the document screen.

9. Be sure to save the document.

The following options are available in the Find and Replace Text dialog box:

- *Replace*. This option replaces the highlighted string with the replacement string, stopping at each occurrence.

- *Find*. This option does not replace the highlighted string but instead finds the next occurrence of the search string.
- *Replace All*. This option replaces all occurrences of the search string.

Exercise 2: Using Find and Replace to Correct Errors

In this exercise you will begin to correct the errors in the Calendar.mem document created in previous units.

1. Retrieve the file Calendar.mem from your floppy disk.

2. Position the cursor at the top of the screen.

3. Make the appropriate menu selections to invoke the Replace feature, and fill in the dialog box so that it looks like figure 4.4.

4. Select Replace All in the dialog box so that all occurrences of "calender" will be replaced with the correct spelling, "calendar."

5. Close the Replace dialog box and examine your document.

6. Save the document.

4.3: To Use the Spell Checker

WordPerfect's *Speller* compares each word in a document to the words in the WordPerfect dictionary. WordPerfect's 115,000-word dictionary contains a file that lists common words (frequently used words) and main words (words generally found in a dictionary). WordPerfect's Speller checks each word against its list of common words first; and if the Speller doesn't find the word there, the program looks in its dictionary of main words. In addition to WordPerfect's dictionary, you also can create a *supplemental dictionary*, in which you can save words that are not in the WordPerfect dictionary.

The Speller can locate three types of errors in a document: misspellings caused by typing errors; double words, such as *the the*; and irregular capitalization, such as *DAte* or *daTE*. Because of the Speller's phonetic capability, you can enter a word exactly as it sounds, such as *okashunaly* for *occasionally*, and the Speller will find the correct spelling in the dictionary.

Checking a Word, a Page, a Document, or a Selection

WordPerfect can check the spelling of the current word, selected text, a sentence, a paragraph, a page, or the entire document. WordPerfect also can check spelling from the insertion point to the end of the page or document, or check spelling for a specified number of pages beginning with the current page.

 STEPS

To use the Speller, follow these steps:

1. Open the **T**ools menu; then choose **S**peller.

    WordPerfect opens the Speller window.

2. Open the Chec**k** menu to specify how much of the document you want WordPerfect to check. The default setting is the entire document.

3. Choose **S**tart.

    WordPerfect begins checking the spelling of each word in the specified section of text.

When selecting the amount of text to check, choose from the following options:

*   *Word*. This option checks the spelling of the word containing the cursor.
*   *Sentence*. This option checks the sentence that contains the cursor.
*   *Paragraph*. This option checks the paragraph that contains the cursor.
*   *Page*. This option checks the page that contains the cursor.
*   *Document*. This option checks the spelling of the entire document.
*   *To End of Document*. This option checks the spelling from the cursor's position to the end of the document.
*   *Selected Text*. This option checks the spelling of the highlighted text.
*   *Text Entry Box*. This option checks the spelling of text that you enter into a text box within a WordPerfect dialog box.
*   *Number of Pages*. This option displays the Number of Pages text entry box, in which you can specify the number of pages to be checked, beginning with the current page.

Selecting an Alternative Spelling

If the Speller finds a word not included in any of the dictionary lists, WordPerfect highlights the word in the document and offers alternative spellings in the Suggestions list box. The message Not Found, followed by the unknown word, appears near the top of the Speller window. Speller also places in the Replace With Text box, the first alternative word listed in the Suggestions list box.

To replace the highlighted word in the document with an alternative spelling, follow these steps: **STEPS**

1. Select an alternative spelling from the Suggestions list box by clicking it (see fig. 4.5).

Fig. 4.5
The Speller displaying the alternative listings from which to choose.

2. Choose the **R**eplace command button.

   WordPerfect replaces the highlighted word with the alternative spelling, and then continues to check the selected text.

    The first alternative spelling is automatically selected when the Suggestions list box appears; simply choose **R**eplace to insert
   TIP this alternative spelling into the document.

Using Command Buttons in the Speller Window

When the Speller window does not display the correct spelling, you can use one of the following options:

- Type what you think is the correct spelling in the Replace **W**ith text box, and choose the S**u**ggest command button.

- Choose the Skip **O**nce command button to have the Speller ignore this particular occurrence of the unknown word in the document.

- Choose the Skip **A**lways command button to have the Speller ignore all occurrences of the unknown word in the document.

- Choose the **Ad**d command button to add the unknown word to the supplementary dictionary.

- Choose the **C**lose command to close the Speller window and cancel the spelling check.

Typing Spelling Changes

Occasionally a word will be too far off the mark for WordPerfect to recognize it as any word at all. When this happens, you will need to type in the correct spelling of the word.

STEPS

To type your own editing changes, follow these steps:

1. Type your own changes into the Replace With text box.

2. Choose Replace.

   The Speller replaces the highlighted word in the text with the word you typed.

Using Other Options in the Speller Window

You can choose several other options from the Options pull-down menu in the Speller window. Options that are checked are turned on, as shown in figure 4.6.

Fig. 4.6
Speller options
which are turned
on are indicated
by a check mark.

The options available from the Options pull-down menu include the following:

- *Words with Numbers*. When your document contains words with numbers such as, *B52* or *RX7*, the Speller stops at each occurrence unless you deselect this option.

- *Duplicate Words*. The Speller searches for double words, such as *the the*, and when it locates double words, the Speller displays the message Duplicate Words. In order to delete one of the duplicates, you must choose Replace. You must deselect this option if you want duplicate words ignored.

- *Irregular Capitalization*. When locating a word with questionable capitalization, the message Capitalization appears, followed by the word in question. To change the capitalization, choose the Replace command. You must deselect this option to ignore occurrences.

- *Auto Replace*. Choose this option to have WordPerfect automatically replace misspelled words.

- *Document Dictionary*. This option enables you to create specialized dictionaries that the Speller uses to check specific documents.

Exercise 3: Using the Spell Checker on the Calendar.mem file

In this exercise you will run the spell check on the Calendar.mem file. The spell checker won't catch all of the errors, but it will find most of the ones that remain.

1. Open the Calendar.mem file, if necessary.

2. Position the cursor at the top of the document.

3. Make the appropriate menu selections to run the spell checker on the entire document.

4. Save the edited document.

4.4: To Use the Thesaurus

WordPerfect's *Thesaurus* can improve your writing by helping you find alternative choices for many common words in your document. The Thesaurus is similar to the Speller, except that the Thesaurus lists alternative word choices instead of alternative spellings.

The Thesaurus contains approximately 10,000 *headwords*. Headwords are words associated with lists of alternative word choices. If the word you are looking up is a headword, WordPerfect displays a list of *synonyms* (words with identical or similar meanings) and *antonyms* (words with opposite meanings). You can choose one of these and substitute it for the selected word in the text. If the word you are looking for is not a headword, the message Word Not Found appears at the bottom of the dialog box.

To replace a word using the Thesaurus, follow these steps:

STEPS

1. Move the cursor to the word you want to look up in the Thesaurus and select the word.

2. Open the Tools menu; then choose Thesaurus.

    WordPerfect displays the Thesaurus dialog box (see fig. 4.7).

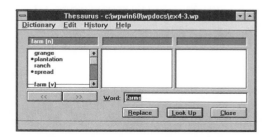

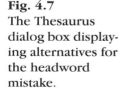
Fig. 4.7
The Thesaurus dialog box displaying alternatives for the headword mistake.

3. Select the alternative word you want to use. The program places it in the **W**ord text box.

4. Choose **Re**place.

   The document reflects the change.

You may not see the exact word you want in the list of alternative words, but you may see a word that is similar to the one you want.

 To see a list of synonyms and antonyms for an alternative headword, follow these steps:

1. Double-click any of the words in the list box that is preceded by a bullet, or select the word and press ⏎Enter. (The bullet preceding a word indicates that it is a headword.)

   Additional choices appear in the list boxes to the right.

2. Select one of the alternative words, and then choose **Re**place.

3. Choose **C**lose to exit the Thesaurus window.

Exercise 4: Using the Thesaurus

In this exercise you will use the Thesaurus to replace a word in the Calendar.mem file.

1. Retrieve the Calendar.mem file if you haven't already done so.

2. Highlight the word "rationale" in the second paragraph and invoke the Thesaurus.

3. Select a word from the suggested list that you think is the most appropriate replacement and complete the replacement process.

4. Save the document.

Using the Look Up Option

If the word you are looking for is not a headword in the Thesaurus, the Thesaurus window will be empty, and you see the message Word not Found in the lower left corner of the Status bar. To look up alternative words, you must enter a synonym of your own in the **W**ord text box; then choose the **L**ook Up command button.

4.5: To Use the Grammar Checker

WordPerfect for Windows includes a powerful grammar checker, called Grammatik, which can help you to identify and correct errors in writing style, grammar, and sentence structure. Grammatik also can check spelling, as well as adapt to 10 different writing styles (informal, business, and so on).

The Options menu in the Grammatik dialog box contains the following options which you can choose to customize your grammar-checking task:

- *Writing Style*. Choose this option to display the Writing Style dialog box that contains 10 supplied writing styles from which to choose.
- *Checking Options*. Choose this option to display the Options dialog box.
- *Grammar, Mechanics and Style*. Choose this option to check for grammar errors specifically related to mechanics and style.
- *Grammar and Mechanics*. Choose this option to check for grammar and mechanical errors, but not for errors in style.
- *Statistics*. Choose this option to display the Document Statistics dialog box, without correcting any spelling and grammar errors. The Document Statistics dialog box shows a list of grammar-related statistics, such as number of sentences, number of words, average words per sentence, and so on.

To use Grammatik to check a document, follow these steps:

STEPS

1. Open the Tools menu; then choose **Grammatik**.

   WordPerfect displays the Grammatik dialog box.

2. Open the Check menu, and choose one of the following options: **Sentence, Paragraph, Document** (the default), To **End** of Document, or Selected **Text**.

3. Choose **Start** to begin checking grammar using the default options set for writing style, grammar, sentence mechanics, and so on.

   When Grammatik encounters a content error, such as a long sentence (see fig. 4.8), you have the following options:

   - Click in the document and make any necessary changes.
   - Choose **Skip** or Next **Sentence** to ignore this error and continue checking the document.

Fig. 4.8
The Grammatik
dialog box.

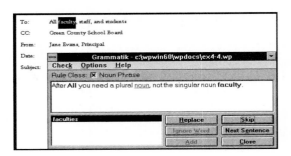

To display information about a specific error, open the
Help menu and choose **Rule Class**. Grammatik displays the
Grammatik 5 Window with specific information about the error.
To return to the dialog box from the Grammatik 5 window, open
the **File** menu, and choose **Exit**. To continue checking a docu-
ment, choose the **Resume** command button.

When Grammatik encounters a spelling error, you can choose
Replace, **Ignore Word**, or **Add**.

4. When you reach the end of a document, WordPerfect displays a
   message asking whether you want to close the grammar checker.
   Choose **Yes** or **No**.

Exercise 5: Using Grammatik on the Calendar.mem file

In this exercise you will run the grammar checker on the memo file to find the
remaining errors.

1. With the Calendar.mem file on the screen, select Grammatik from the
   menu.

2. Start the grammar checker.

3. Make corrections for each error in the document. In some instances,
   the style of the memo or conversational phrasing conventions will
   supercede the strict rules applied by the grammar checker. In other
   words, you make the call!

4. Notice the problem that Grammatik has with the "are state" phrase.
   Click in the document and change "are" to "our" to make the sentence
   correct. Resume the grammar checker.

5. When the grammar checker has finished, close the window and save
   your document.

6. Exit WordPerfect at this time or continue with the Testing Your Skills 1 section, which follows this unit.

Unit Summary

In this unit, you have learned how to delete hidden codes from the Reveal Codes window and how to use the various tools in WordPerfect 6.0 for Windows, including the Speller, the Thesaurus, and Grammatik.

New Terms

To check your knowledge of the new terms in this unit, consult the glossary at the end of this book.

- Antonym
- Dictionary
- Headword
- String
- Synonym

Testing Your Skills 1

You have decided that it's time to start looking for a computer. In doing research on brands and capabilities, you've come up with a list of system specifications that will meet your needs. Enter the basic document shown below, then make the changes suggested in the numbered steps.

Computer System Specifications for <your name here>.

Intended uses of system: word processing, desktop publishing, small databases, financial planning and budgeting.

Budget:	$2500-$3000
System Specifications:	
Monitor:	15" SVGA Color (17" preferred)
Printer:	Letter quality
Speed:	1-2 ppm
Type:	InkJet or Bubble Jet
Interface:	Parallel
Memory:	1 MG
Processor:	80486
Speed:	33 or 66 MHz
RAM:	8-16 MG
Hard drive:	160 MG
Floppy drive:	1.44 MG 3.5"
CD ROM:	Optional

1. Replace the <your name here> marker with your real name.

2. In the "intended uses of system" section, make each use item an indented, bulleted item in a vertical list. (Remember to use the Coach if you need help with this.)

3. Move the third section, which deals with the type of system unit, so that it is the first section in the system specifications description.

4. Spell check the document.

5. Using the Thesaurus, find an alternative for each occurrence of the word "specification."

6. Using the Find and Replace feature, replace all occurrences of the incorrect abbreviation MG with the correct abbreviation for megabyte, MB.

7. Save the document as COMPSEC.XXX, where the three Xs are replaced by your three initials.

8. Print the document.

5

Formatting Paragraphs and Characters

Formatting refers to the appearance of text in a finished document. As a WYSIWYG (What You See Is What You Get) word processing program, WordPerfect can display on-screen almost all of the formatting you use in your document.

Formatting occurs on three levels in a WordPerfect document: the page level, the paragraph level, and the character level. In WordPerfect for Windows, you can perform most paragraph and character formatting in the document editing window by using the Ruler and the Power Bar. This chapter introduces you to the formatting capabilities of WordPerfect for Windows which include changing margin settings, creating tab settings, and using different types of indentation, alignments, and justification.

5.1: To Set Margins

WordPerfect's default margin setting is one inch for both the left and the right margins. You can change these settings by using the Ruler or the Margins dialog box.

Adjusting the Left and Right Margins by Using the Ruler

The top line of the Ruler indicates the document margins. This part of the Ruler contains triangles pointing toward each other, which represent the left and right margin settings. The shaded areas on the left and right side of the bar depict the actual margins, that is, the distance between the edge of the paper and the margin setting (see fig. 5.1).

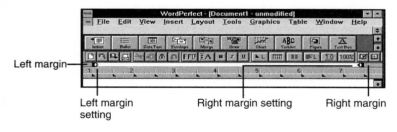

Fig. 5.1
Left and right margin settings and the left and right margins are shown on the Ruler.

As shown in figure 5.1, for a page width setting of 8 1/2 inches, the WordPerfect default places the left margin setting at the 1-inch mark, and the right margin setting at the 7 1/2-inch mark on the Ruler.

To change the left margin to 1 1/2 inches by using the Ruler, perform the following steps:

STEPS

1. Display the Ruler Bar by choosing the **View** menu; then choose **Ruler Bar**.

2. Position the mouse pointer over the icon representing the left margin in the Ruler Bar.

3. Drag the left margin icon to the 1 1/2-inch mark on the Ruler.

   Notice the dotted line that appears as you drag the icon to its new position (see fig. 5.2).

4. Release the mouse button.

   As soon as you reset a margin, WordPerfect immediately reflows the text of your document from the cursor position forward to conform to the new setting.

Fig. 5.2
Dragging the left
margin icon to a
new setting.

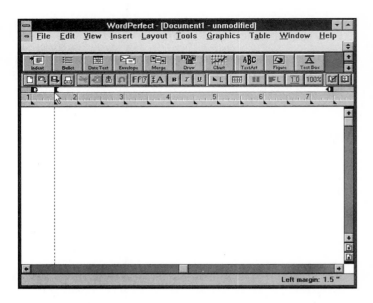

Using the Margins Dialog Box

You also can change the left and right margin settings by typing new values
into the **Left** and **Right** text boxes in the Margins dialog box.

 STEPS

To display the Margins dialog box using the Ruler and then change the right
margin to 1 1/2 inches, perform the following steps:

1. Double-click anywhere in the margin area (the gray portion) of the
   Ruler or on the margin icon.

   WordPerfect displays the Margins dialog box.

2. Click in the **Right** text box, type the new margin dimension, and then
   press ⮐Enter or click OK.

   NOTE

   You also can scroll through the list box to view the different
   measurements available, and choose 1.50 from the list box.

Exercise 1: Setting the Margins of a Page

In this exercise you will set the margins for a new document. Each subsequent
exercise in this unit will build upon the previous exercise.

1. Start WordPerfect and open a new document, if necessary.

2. Using whichever margin setting method you prefer, set the left margin at 1.5 and the right margin at 1.0.

3. Save the document as **Money.ltr**, but leave the document on-screen.

5.2: To Set Tabs

WordPerfect's default tab ruler positions left-justified tab stops at half-inch intervals. WordPerfect supports four types of tab settings: left, center, right, and decimal (see table 5.1).

Table 5.1 Types of Tab Settings Available in WordPerfect	
Type	*Effect on Text*
Left	Left-justifies text at the tab stop. In Insert mode, WordPerfect indents existing text to the tab stop. The left tab is the default.
Center	Centers text at the tab stop. A center tab is commonly used to center column headings in tables.
Right	Right-justifies text at the tab stop.
Decimal	Justifies text on the alignment character (by default, the period) at the tab stop so that any text typed before the period is right-justified, and any text typed after the period is left-justified. A decimal tab is often used to align columns of numbers on the decimal point.

Each type of tab is represented by a different marker in the Ruler, and each can include a *dot leader*, a series of periods preceding the tab. The Tab pulldown menu accessed from the Power Bar describes each kind of tab available. (see fig. 5.3).

Fig. 5.3
Tab options from
the Power Bar.

Unit 5: Formatting Paragraphs and Characters

 STEPS To change a single tab setting by using the Ruler, follow these steps:

1. Place the mouse pointer on the tab you want changed and drag it off the Ruler Bar.

2. Position the mouse pointer in the Tab Ruler, and click the right mouse button to display the QuickMenu which contains the different tab types, (see fig. 5.4).

Fig. 5.4
The Tab Ruler
QuickMenu,
displaying
different
tab types.

3. Choose the type of tab you want, with or without dot leaders, from the QuickMenu.

4. Use the mouse pointer to select the position on the Tab Ruler where you want to insert the tab, and click the left mouse button. When you release the left mouse button, the new tab marker appears on the Ruler.

 STEPS To create additional tabs and place them on the Ruler, perform the following steps:

1. Position the mouse pointer in the Tab Ruler, and click the right mouse button to display the QuickMenu or click the Tab Set button on the Power Bar to display a drop-down menu of tab types.

2. Choose Clear All Tabs from the QuickMenu to remove all the default tab settings from the Ruler Bar.

3. Position the mouse pointer in the Tab Ruler, and click the right mouse button to display the QuickMenu.

4. Choose Right to select a right tab setting. Release the mouse button.

5. Position the pointer at the desired location on the Tab Ruler. (Make sure the pointer is under the very thin line that separates the tab area from the numbered area).

6. Click the left mouse button to place the right tab on the Tab Ruler.

7. Practice using this method by inserting a center tab at position 2.5", a decimal tab at position 3.5", a left dot leader tab at position 4.5", and a right dot leader tab at position 5.5".

If you accidentally place the tab in the wrong location, drag it to the correct location.

Using the Tab Set Dialog Box

You can use the Tab Set dialog box to delete all existing tabs, to set precise increments for tab stops, or to set a series of uniformly spaced tabs across the ruler.

To display the Tab Set dialog box when the Ruler is displayed, follow these steps:

1. Position the mouse pointer on any tab stop on the Tab Ruler, and double-click the left mouse button. WordPerfect displays the Tab Set dialog box.

2. Choose the tab Type, Position and other options from the Tab Set dialog box.

Exercise 2: Setting the Tabs

In this exercise you will set the tab stops for the Money.ltr file.

1. In the Money.ltr file, clear all preset tabs.

2. Set a left tab at 2.0".

3. Set a left tab with dot leaders at 5.0".

4. Set a decimal tab at 6.5".

5. Save the document.

5.3: To Indent Paragraphs

When you use WordPerfect's Tab or Indent feature, the settings in your document control how the text of a paragraph is indented. When you press Tab↹ or choose Indent, WordPerfect inserts a hidden code that indents the text to the next available tab setting. Do not use spaces to indent text in a document because your text will not align properly when printed.

Indenting Paragraphs by Using a Tab

If you want to indent only the first line of a paragraph from the left margin, you can just press Tab↹. Each time you press Tab↹, the cursor moves to the next tab stop on the Ruler.

In order to indent existing text by pressing $\boxed{\text{Tab}^{\updownarrow}}$, you must be in Insert mode with your cursor placed immediately before the first letter of the line you want to indent.

Indenting a Paragraph on the Left

You can use WordPerfect's Indent feature to indent an entire paragraph instead of just the first line.

 STEPS
To indent an entire paragraph from the left margin, follow these steps:

1. Open the Layout menu.

2. Choose Paragraph; then choose Indent. The cursor moves to the next tab stop, temporarily resetting the left margin. All text you type until you press $\boxed{\text{←Enter}}$ is indented to this tab stop (see fig. 5.5). Use the same steps to indent an existing paragraph, but make sure that the cursor is located at the beginning of the paragraph, and that the Status Bar indicates that you are in Insert mode.

Fig. 5.5
WordPerfect
supports
multiple types
of indentation.

Tab-indented paragraph

Paragraph using Indent

Double indented paragraph

Paragraph using hanging indent

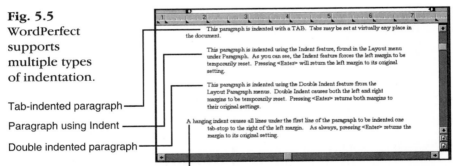

Indenting a Paragraph on the Left and Right

When you want to indent text from both margins, you can choose the Double Indent option.

 STEPS
To indent a paragraph from both the left and the right margins, follow these steps:

1. Open the Layout menu.

2. Choose Paragraph; then choose Double Indent. The cursor moves to the next tab stop, and the left and right margins are reset temporarily. All text you type is indented one tab stop on the left and one tab stop on the right until you press $\boxed{\text{←Enter}}$.

Creating a Hanging Indent

A *hanging indent* places the first line of a paragraph flush with the left margin, and indents to the first tab stop all subsequent lines of the paragraph. Entries in a bibliography frequently use a hanging indent.

To create a hanging indent for a new paragraph, perform the following steps: **STEPS**

1. Position the cursor at the beginning of a new line.

2. Open the Layout menu.

3. Choose Paragraph; then choose Hanging Indent.

4. Enter text for the paragraph.

Changing the Type of Justification

Justification determines the way in which the lines in each paragraph are aligned. Table 5.2 describes the five types of justification that WordPerfect supports.

Table 5.2 Types of Justification Available in WordPerfect	
Option	*Effect on Text*
Left	Justifies text on the left margin, leaving a ragged-right margin. Left is the default justification for all new documents.
Right	Justifies text on the right margin, leaving a ragged-left margin.
Center	Centers all lines of text.
Full	Justifies text on the left and right margins, except the last line of the paragraph.
All	Justifies text on the left and right margins, including the last line of the paragraph. Enables you to evenly space letters in a title or a heading between the left and right margins.

To change the type of justification in a document, follow these steps: **STEPS**

1. Position the mouse pointer on the Justification button on the Power Bar.

> **!** **TIP** As you move the mouse across the icons of the Power Bar, the top line of the screen indicates what each icon represents.

2. While pointing to the Justification icon, press and hold down the left mouse button. A pop-up list of justification choices appears.

3. While holding down the mouse button, highlight the justification option you want, and release the mouse button to choose the option. WordPerfect realigns the text according to the justification used.

TIP To apply a justification type to only one section of text, select the section of text before using the preceding steps.

Exercise 3: Entering and Formatting Text

In this exercise you will begin a letter to your rich Aunt Helga, asking for money to help pay for spring terms costs.

1. Open the document **Money.ltr** if it is not already open.

2. Enter the letter shown in figure 5.6.

Fig. 5.6
Text for Money.ltr document.

> January 1, 1994
>
> Ima Beggar
> 2271 Mooch Court,
> Apartment IO
> Indebted, OR 97401
>
> Mrs. Chester Gotbuchs
> Two Uome Street
> Richland, NY 12002
>
> Dear Aunt Helga:
>
> I am writing to ask for a loan so that I can finish my senior year in college and graduate on time. I have been working part time for the last two years and have been able to make ends meet each semester. However, my required course load for spring graduatation prohibits me from working this semester. Thus, I am caught in the system. If I work, I won't graduate. If I don't work, I can't afford to graduate. I have prepared a simple listing of my budget this semester, so that you can examine my expenses. I will be interviewing this spring for jobs and feel confident that I will be able to pay you back within a year from the time I graduate.
>
> | | |
> |---|---|
> | Tuition . . . . | $2,000.00 |
> | Books . . . . | $350.00 |
> | Room and Board . . . . | $2,600.00 |
> | Miscellaneous Expenses . . . . | $600.00 |
> | Total: . . . . | $5,550.00 |
>
> Thanks in advance for any help you can provide me with.
>
> Sincerely,
> Ima

3. Change the justification of the main paragraph to full.

4. Save the document.

5.4: To Align Text

When you enter a report title or heading, you may want to modify the alignment of a single short line. You can choose to center a line of text between the margins, center text on a specific point in a line, or align the text flush with the right margin.

To center a heading between the left and right margins of a document, perform the following steps:

1. Place the cursor on line you wish to center. The line may be blank or have text already entered into it.

2. Open the Layout menu.

3. Choose Line; then choose Center. The cursor moves to the center of the page.

4. If the line was blank, type in new text and press ⏎Enter). Notice that the text is inserted from the right to the left as you type.

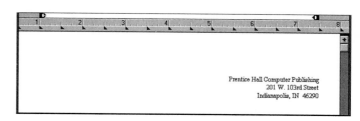

Fig. 5.7
A return address flush right.

Prentice Hall Computer Publishing
201 W. 103rd Street
Indianapolis, IN 46290

Aligning Flush Right

You can easily align individual lines of text with the right margin when using WordPerfect. This technique is useful when you want to enter a return address flush right in a business letter (see fig. 5.7).

To align the text flush right as you type it, perform the following steps:

1. Position the cursor at the top of the document.

2. Open the Layout menu.

3. Choose Line, and then choose Flush Right. The cursor moves to the right margin.

4. Type the text and press ⏎Enter). Notice that the text is entered from right to the left as you type.

To right-align existing text, simply position the cursor at the beginning of the line before executing steps 2 and 3.

Aligning Text on a Decimal or Other Character

Aligning numbers is the most common use for aligning text using the Decimal Align feature. Numbers often look best when they are aligned along the decimal points, especially if all the numbers in the column do not have the same number of digits. In some instances, you may want to align text along another character, such as a dollar sign.

Using Decimal Align

 STEPS

To align text on a decimal or other alignment character, follow these steps:

1. Position the cursor at the beginning of a blank line.

2. Press Tab⇥ to move the cursor to a position where you have set a decimal tab stop.

3. Type the text that precedes the alignment character. All text moves to the left of the decimal tab stop until you type the alignment character.

4. Type the alignment character (such as the period) followed by any text that follows. All text typed after the alignment character moves to the right of the tab stop.

Exercise 4: Aligning the Closing

In this exercise you will align the closing of the Money.ltr letter flush right.

1. Place the cursor in front of the S in Sincerely.

2. Select the appropriate menu choices to align the line flush right.

3. Place the cursor in front of the I in Ima and align the line flush right.

4. Save the document.

5.5: To Enhance Text

One method of enhancing text is to use various fonts. A *font* is a collection of characters with an identifiable typeface, such as Courier or Times Roman. In WordPerfect, you can adjust the font, size, and appearance (or attribute) of text. You can choose from *proportionally spaced* fonts (different characters take up different amounts of horizontal space on the line) or *monospaced* fonts (each character takes up the same amount of space on the line).

WordPerfect uses point size to determine basic character height. A *point* is the fundamental measure of type. Because 72 points equal one inch, 72-point Times Roman characters, for example, are approximately one inch tall.

The printer you use determines, to a large extent, the number of fonts available to you in WordPerfect. When you begin a new document, WordPerfect uses the font designated as the initial font for the printer you are using. (When you choose a new printer, this initial font usually changes.)

Open a new document window to complete the following exercises.

Choosing a Font

To choose a font for a document, perform the following steps:

STEPS

1. Position the cursor at the top of the document.

2. Open the Layout menu, and choose Font. The Font dialog box appears (see fig. 5.8).

Fig. 5.8
The Font dialog box.

3. Choose the font you want to use from the Font Face list box. You can preview your chosen font in the Resulting Font box. The sample text also reflects any modifications you make to the point size or appearance attributes.

4. To change the size of your new font, type the desired point size into the Font Size box, or choose a size from the Font Size list box.

5. To add attributes to the font, choose the desired options from the Appearance, Position, and Relative Size boxes.

6. When you are satisfied with the appearance of the sample text in the Resulting Font box, choose OK to apply the changes.

You can apply different fonts and attributes to new or existing text. To change existing text, you must select the text you want to modify before you open the Font dialog box and execute the steps outlined.

Applying Attributes to Text

You may want to enhance a heading with boldfaced type or indicate the title of a periodical or book by making the title italic. You can apply these types of attributes to your text as you enter the text or after you enter text.

Adding Bold, Italic, and Underline Attributes to Text

STEPS

To make the text in your document boldfaced, underlined, or italicized, perform the following steps:

1. Highlight the text you wish to enhance.

2. Open the Layout menu; then choose Font.

3. Choose **Bold** (or Underline or Italic) from the Appearance box, and then choose OK. The font name in the Status bar is displayed in boldface, indicating that Bold is on.

4. Click the mouse button to see the boldfaced text in your document.

5. Repeat steps 1 and 2; then choose Bold in the Appearance box to remove the boldfacing. (The X should be removed from the check box next to the attribute name.) The font name on the Status bar returns to normal, indicating that Bold is off.

Your choice of font type and appearance is limited by the capabilities of your printer.

You also can assign attributes to text before you type by executing steps 2 and 3 in the steps above before typing text into your document.

Removing Attributes

STEPS

To remove attributes applied to the text, follow these steps:

1. Select the text for which you want to remove an attribute.

2. Open the Font dialog box.

3. Choose any attributes that are currently applied to the text, so that the X is removed from the check box beside the attribute.

Alternatively, you can select **R**eveal Codes from the **V**iew menu and delete the enhancement code there.

Using Superscript and Subscript

Superscript and subscript also are available in the Font dialog box. *Superscript* prints a character in a smaller point size and above the normal line of text. *Subscript* prints a character below the normal line of text, and if possible, in a smaller point size (see fig. 5.9).

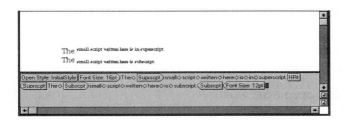

Fig. 5.9
A document using superscript and subscript.

Applying Superscript and Subscript

To apply superscript and subscript features, follow these steps:

1. Open the Layout menu, and choose **F**ont. WordPerfect displays the Font dialog box.

2. Click and hold down the mouse button on the arrow in the position box. WordPerfect displays options.

3. Choose **P**osition and S**u**perscript (or Su**b**script); then choose OK.

4. Type the character or characters you want to appear as superscript or subscript text. WordPerfect shows the characters you type above or below the baseline of the regular text.

5. To turn off the options and return text to normal, repeat steps 1 and 2.

Changing the Line Spacing

By default, WordPerfect uses single-spacing for each new document you create. You can change this default by increasing or decreasing the line spacing by half-line increments.

STEPS

To change the line spacing from single-spacing to double-spacing by using the Power Bar, follow these steps:

1. Click the Line Spacing button on the Power Bar and hold down the left mouse button until the pop-up menu containing line spacing options appears.

 TIP As you move the mouse across the icons of the Power Bar, the top line of the screen indicates what each icon represents.

2. Drag down the list until the number *2* is highlighted.

3. Release the mouse button to put the line spacing into effect. The icon on the Power Bar now reflects the changed spacing. A line spacing code [Ln Spacing] is inserted into the document at the location of the cursor.(You can see the code in the Reveal Codes window.) The code affects any text typed from this point to the end of the document or until WordPerfect encounters another [Ln Spacing] code.

Exercise 5: Enhancing the Letter

In this exercise you will add emphasis to certain words in the letter by using enhancement features.

1. With the Money.ltr document on the screen, move the cursor to the I in "If I work, ...".

2. Select the sentences: "If I work, I won't graduate. If I don't work, I can't afford to graduate."

3. Underline those sentences to add emphasis.

4. Change the line spacing in the main paragraph to 1.5, so that the letter will be easier for your elderly Aunt Helga to read.

5. To encourage Aunt Helga to fund your entire semester, boldface the word *Total:* in the budget.

6. Save the document.

5.6: To Control Line Breaks

WordPerfect offers several features to help you control how and when a line breaks in a paragraph. The most commonly used method is the Hyphenation feature. You can use this feature to hyphenate words and reduce the raggedness of the right margin when your document is left-justified or reduce the amount of white space between words when using full justification.

Keeping Text Together with Hard Spaces

WordPerfect generally breaks the end of a line at the space between the last word that will fit and the next word. In some cases, however, you may want to keep two words together, such as a date (January 11, 1994). To prevent words from separating on different lines, you can enter a hard space between the pair of words to bind them together. To enter a hard space, press Ctrl + Spacebar .

Hyphenating Text Manually

You can manually hyphenate words by entering any of the following types of hyphens supported by WordPerfect:

- *Hard Hyphen.* Press - to separate compound words that always require hyphenation, such as *self-defense* and *mother-in-law*. Use a hard hyphen when you don't care whether word wrap separates the words on different lines. Hard hyphens are always visible in the document and are always printed.

- *Dash Character.* Press Ctrl + - to bind together hyphenated words into one unit so that WordPerfect wraps the entire unit to the next line when it extends beyond the right margin. Use dash characters on text that should always stay together on a line, such as dates (07-05-93) or products (Lotus 1-2-3).

- *Soft Hyphen.* Press Ctrl + ⇧Shift + - to indicate where a word should be hyphenated when that word extends beyond the right margin. When the word does not extend beyond the right margin, the hyphen is not visible and is not printed. WordPerfect inserts this type of hyphenation when you use the automatic Hyphenation feature.

Turning On the Hyphenation Feature

By default, WordPerfect's Hyphenation feature is turned off.

To turn on Hyphenation in order to control line spacing, follow these steps:

STEPS

1. Move to the beginning of the document you want to hyphenate.

2. Open the Layout menu, and choose Line; then choose Hyphenation. WordPerfect displays the Line Hyphenation dialog box (see fig. 5.10).

3. Turn on Hyphenation by choosing the Hyphenation **On** check box.

4. Choose OK.

You can use the Hyphenation feature in two ways. You can turn on the Hyphenation feature and make hyphenation decisions as you type the text of a document; or you can enter all the text first and then go to the beginning of the document, turn on Hyphenation, and scroll through the document to hyphenate it.

Fig. 5.10
The Line Hyphen-
ation dialog box.

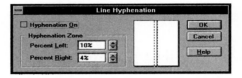

Unit Summary

In this unit, you have learned many ways to format paragraphs and characters in WordPerfect for Windows by using the Ruler and dialog boxes. You also have learned how to use the hyphenation options, as well as how to use text attributes and line spacing.

New Terms

To check your knowledge of the new terms in this unit, consult the glossary at the end of this book.

- Font
- Line height
- Ruler

Formatting Pages

6

Unit 5 discussed formatting documents at the paragraph and character levels. Formatting at the paragraph level affects the layout of each paragraph of text; and formatting at the character level affects the font, size, and type styles assigned to individual characters and words.

This unit examines formatting at the page level. When formatting at the page level, you are primarily concerned with the overall layout of the page and any recurring elements in the design. In this unit, you learn how to choose paper size and type; how to add headers, footers, and page numbers; and how to control page breaks in a document.

6.1: To Choose Paper Definitions

A paper definition includes information on the size of the paper, paper type (the name assigned to the paper definition), the location of the paper in the printer

Objectives

When you have finished this chapter, you will have learned the following:

6.1 To Choose Paper Definitions

6.2 To Change Margins and Center Text Vertically

6.3 To Work with Headers and Footers

6.4 To Number Pages

6.5 To Control Page Breaks

(continuous, bin, or manual feed), and the orientation of the printing on the page (portrait or landscape). WordPerfect comes with several predefined forms, including Standard, Labels, and Envelopes that can be used with most printers. Paper definitions are directly related to the printer you are using and are therefore limited to that printer's capabilities.

WordPerfect's default paper size is Standard, which uses 8 1/2-by-11-inch paper in *Portrait mode* (where text runs parallel to the shorter side of the paper). If you want to use a different paper size or intend to change the orientation to *Landscape mode* (where text runs parallel to the longer side of the paper), you can choose a different paper size for your document.

You can base your paper definition on one of the predefined sizes in the **S**ize list or create your own size by using the User Defined Size option. The **S**ize list contains the following options:

- Letter   8 1/2 inches by 11 inches
- Legal   8 1/2 inches by 14 inches
- Executive   7 1/4 inches by 10 1/2 inches
- A4   210 mm by 297 mm
- B5   182 mm by 257 mm
- Envelope # 10   4 1/8 inches by 9 1/2 inches
- User Defined Size   Type a width and length in the **B**y text boxes.

 To choose a paper size for a document, perform the following steps:

1. Position the cursor at the top of the page where you want the new paper size to take effect.

2. Open the **L**ayout menu, choose **P**age, and then choose Paper **S**ize. WordPerfect displays the Paper Size dialog box with a list of paper definitions.

3. Select a paper definition in the **P**aper Definitions list box by highlighting the definition. The picture in the Orientation box reflects the different choices of paper definitions as you go through them.

4. Choose the **S**elect command button to put the new paper size into effect and return to the document.

Choosing Envelope Definitions

WordPerfect's Envelope option enables you to create new envelope definitions or customize existing envelope definitions (see fig. 6.1).

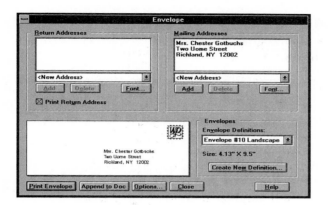

Fig. 6.1
The Envelope dialog box displaying a graphic of the automatically addressed envelope.

The following options are available in the Envelope dialog box:

- **Add.** This option adds the address displayed in the **M**ailing Addresses list to a stored list of addresses you frequently print on envelopes. The program lists the first line of each address in the box below the mailing addresses box. To choose an address from this list, select it and press (⏎Enter).

- **Return Addresses.** You can type a return address in this space. WordPerfect shows the position of the return address in the sample envelope window. You can store this address for future use by choosing the **A**dd button.

- **Print Return Address.** Select this check box if you want to print the return address; remove the X if you want to omit the return address.

- **Envelope Definition.** Choose this option, and select a new envelope definition from the drop-down list.

- **Create New Definition.** This button displays the Create Envelope Definition dialog box, where you can specify a new envelope paper size, type, and location, as well as the envelope printer orientation.

- **Print Envelope.** Choose this button to print the document and return to the document window.

- **Append to Doc.** This option moves the insertion point to the end of the current document, inserts a hard page break, and inserts the envelope definition and text. This option is useful when you want to save an envelope definition with a document.

- **Options.** You choose this option to display the Envelope Options dialog box, where you can adjust the position of the mailing and return addresses.

Addressing an Envelope Automatically

WordPerfect can automatically read the address from a letter on-screen and then print the address on the envelope.

 STEPS

To have WordPerfect automatically address an envelope, perform the following steps:

1. Open an existing letter or create an address in a new document.

2. Position the cursor on or above the address in the letter.

3. Open the Layout menu, and choose Envelope. WordPerfect displays a sample graphic in the bottom left corner of the Envelope dialog box to show you how the printed envelope will look (refer to fig. 6.1).

4. Choose Close to return to the document window.

Exercise 1: Creating an Envelope for Money.ltr

In this exercise you will create an envelope in which to mail the Money.ltr file.

1. With Money.ltr open, place the cursor in the mailing address text.

2. Click on the envelope Power button from the Power Bar or make the appropriate menu selection to activate the envelope dialog box.

3. Check to make sure that the addressee's name and address appear in the right place in the dialog box.

4. Enter your name and address in the return address box.

5. Click on Append to Doc to have the envelope appended to the document.

6. Close the envelope dialog box and save the file.

6.2: To Change Margins and Center Text Vertically

By default, WordPerfect sets all four page margins at one inch. As you learned in Unit 5, "Formatting Paragraphs and Characters," you can use the Ruler to change the left and right margins. To change the top and bottom margins, however, you must use the Margins dialog box.

Changing Top and Bottom Page Margins

To change the top and bottom page margins of a document, perform the following steps:

1. Position the cursor on the page where you want the new margins to take effect.

2. Open the Layout menu, and choose Margins. The Margins dialog box appears (see fig. 6.2).

Fig. 6.2
The Margins
dialog box.

3. To change the top margin, choose the Top text box; then enter the new value.

4. To change the bottom margin, choose the Bottom text box; then enter the new value.

 If your document contains more than one page, you must move the cursor to the beginning of the document to change the margins for the entire document.

5. Choose OK to put the new margins into effect and return to the document.

Centering Text Vertically

Centering text between the top and bottom margins of a page is easy in WordPerfect. You can use this technique when you create a title page that vertically centers the title, byline, and a few lines of explanatory text, for example.

To center text vertically, follow these steps:

1. Position the cursor on the area of the page that contains the text you want to center vertically.

2. Open the Layout menu, and choose Page; then choose Center. The Center Page(s) dialog box appears.

3. Choose Current Page to center just the page containing the cursor.

Choose Current and Subsequent Pages to center all pages from the current page forward, or choose No Centering to turn off page centering.

4. Choose OK to put the centering into effect and return to the document window.

Exercise 2: Working with Margins and Centering Text

In this exercise you will create a rummage sale sign.

1. Open a new document in WordPerfect.

2. Set the left and right margins to .5.

3. Set the top and bottom margins to .5.

4. Select a large, clear font (suggest Helvetica 24). Boldface the font selection for further emphasis.

5. Make the appropriate selections to center the current page.

6. Set the justification to center.

7. Enter the following text:

> **Huge 3-Family Garage Sale**
>
> March 15-18
>
> 7:30am to 5:00pm
>
> 837 Windfree Court
>
> Tons of Baby and Toddler clothing and supplies
>
> Housewares, small appliances
>
> Upright Piano, Pool Table
>
>
> Free Cookies and Punch

8. Save the document as **SALE.SGN**.

6.3: To Work with Headers and Footers

A *header* is information (text or graphics) that prints at the top of every page. A *footer* is information that prints at the bottom of every page (see fig. 6.3).

WordPerfect inserts one blank line between the text on the page and the header or footer. Typical header or footer information may include the unit or section title, page number, and revision dates and times. Header or footer text can consist of several lines; WordPerfect adjusts the text to make the necessary space for them. You also can suppress the header or footer from appearing on every page.

You can create two different headers (Headers A and B) and two different footers (Footers A and B) in the same document. Both Headers A and B, and Footers A and B can appear on every page; however, you must format each header and each footer so that the text of A does not overlap the text of B.

 You cannot see the headers and footers in a document when you are in Draft view, but you can see them in Page view.

Fig. 6.3
A document page that uses both a header and a footer.

Creating a Header or Footer

To create a header or footer, perform the following steps:

1. Position the cursor on the page where you want the header or footer to appear. If you want the header or footer to appear on all pages, move the cursor to the beginning of the document.

2. Open the Layout menu, and choose **H**eader/Footer.

   The Headers/Footers dialog box appears.

3. Indicate whether you are creating your first header (Header **A**), second header (Header **B**), first footer (**F**ooter A), or second footer (**F**ooter B) by choosing the appropriate option button under Select.

4. Choose **C**reate. WordPerfect displays the Header/Footer feature bar beneath the Power Bar (see fig. 6.4).

Fig. 6.4
The Header/
Footer Feature
bar is displayed
beneath the
Power Bar.

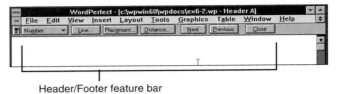

Header/Footer feature bar

The Header/Footer feature bar includes the following options:

- *Number*. Use this option to insert a page number, section number, unit number, or volume number into a header or footer.
- *Line*. Use this option to create a custom graphics line in a header or footer.
- *Placement*. Use this option to place headers or footers on odd pages only, even pages only, or every page.
- *Distance*. Use this option to set the distance between the text and the header or footer.
- *Next*. Use this option to place the cursor at the next header or footer.
- *Previous*. Use this option to place the cursor at the previous header or footer.
- *Close*. Use this option to close the Header/Footer feature bar and return to the document window.

5. Choose Pla**c**ement. WordPerfect displays the Placement dialog box.

6. Choose the Every Page option button, and click OK.

7. Type the header text, and place any graphics you want to appear in the header or footer in the document screen.

8. To insert a page number into the header, choose Nu**m**ber from the Header/Footer feature bar, and then choose Page Number.

9. Choose **C**lose from the feature bar to remove the Header/Footer feature bar.

Editing a Header or Footer

To change the text or appearance of text in a header or a footer, perform the following steps:

1. Open the Layout menu; then choose Header/Footer. The Headers/Footers dialog box appears.

2. Choose the header or footer you want to edit; then choose the **Edit** command button. The feature bar appears enabling you to make any necessary editing changes to the header or footer.

3. Make the necessary changes.

4. Choose Close to record the changes and close the window.

 You can quickly display the Header/Footer feature bar by displaying Reveal Codes (pressing Alt + F3) and double-clicking the header's or footer's hidden code.

Stopping the Printing of a Header or Footer

To stop the printing of a particular header or footer at some point in the document, follow these steps:

1. Position the cursor somewhere on the first page you want to print without the header or footer.

2. Open the Layout menu, and then choose Header/Footer.

3. Choose **Discontinue** from the Headers/Footers dialog box.

Exercise 3: Adding a Header and Footer to the Sale Sign

In this exercise you will add the "small print" to your sign in the form of a header and footer.

1. With the Sale.sgn file on screen, make menu selections to create a header A.

2. Enter the following text as header A text: **Sale.sgn.** This will help you remember what you named the file if you need to edit the sign once you've printed it out.

3. Make menu selections to create a footer A and enter the text: **Cash and local checks only. No bank cards accepted.** Click Close to close the footer window.

STEPS

4. Examine the document in Page view.

5. Edit the footer text so that it says **credit cards** rather than bank cards.

6. Save the document.

6.4: To Number Pages

WordPerfect's Page Numbering feature enables you to place the page number at either the top or bottom margin so that the page number is flush with the left or right margin, or centered. When copying a document on both sides of the page, you can specify that the page numbers alternate between left and right for even and odd pages. You also can use the Page Numbering feature to change the starting page number, change the page text or accompanying symbol type, force a page to be odd or even, or insert the current page number somewhere in the text on that page.

Adding and Formatting Page Numbers

STEPS

To use the Page Numbering feature, perform the following steps:

1. Position the cursor somewhere on the page where you want page numbering to begin. To number the entire document, position the cursor at the beginning of the document.

2. Open the Layout menu, and choose **Page**; then choose **Numbering**. The Page Numbering dialog box is displayed (see fig. 6.5).

Fig. 6.5
The Page
Numbering
dialog box.

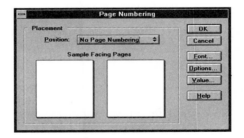

3. By default, No Page Numbering is chosen. To start page numbering, choose one of the options in the **P**osition pop-up list: Top **L**eft, Top **C**enter, Top **R**ight, **A**lternating Top, **B**ottom Left, B**o**ttom Center, Bottom Right, or Alternating Bottom.

As soon as you choose an option, WordPerfect illustrates the page number position in the Sample Facing Pages area in the dialog box.

4. Make your final selection and click OK.

Setting a New Number for a Page

You can begin page numbering at any page in the document; the change will take effect from that page forward. You can choose to start the new page numbering on a new page, a new unit, or on volume numbers. Unit and volume numbers enable you to number larger portions of your document.

To set a new page number, follow these steps:

1. Position the cursor on the page where the numbering is to begin.

2. Open the Layout menu, and choose Page; then choose Numbering.

3. Choose the Value command button from the Page Numbering dialog

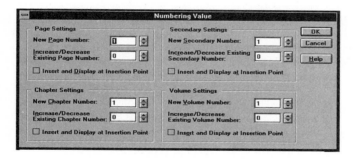

Fig. 6.6
The Numbering
Value dialog box.

box. The Numbering Value dialog box appears (see fig. 6.6).

4. Choose New Page Number in the area for Page, Chapter, Secondary or Volume Settings; then type the starting page number, or scroll to a new page number in the text box.

5. Choose OK to return to the Page Numbering dialog box.

Changing the Numbering Style

You can change the way numbers appear, for example, from Arabic to Roman numerals, by doing the following:

1. From the Page Numbering dialog box, choose the Options command button. WordPerfect displays the Page Numbering Options dialog box (see fig. 6.7).

Fig. 6.7
The Page
Numbering
Options
dialog box.

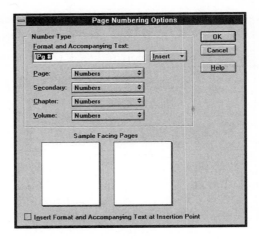

2. Choose a numbering style from the pop-up list for **P**age, **S**econdary, **C**hapter, or **V**olume, and then choose OK to return to the Page Numbering dialog box.

3. Choose OK to return to the document window.

Stopping Page Numbering

STEPS

To stop page numbering at a certain page in the document, follow these steps:

1. Position the cursor on the page where the numbering should stop.

2. Return to the Page Numbering dialog box.

3. Choose the **N**o Page Numbering option under **P**osition.

4. Choose OK. To see how page numbers will look when printed, you must be in Page view; page numbers are not displayed in Draft view.

Suppressing Page Numbering for a Single Page

STEPS

To suppress page numbering, as well as headers and footers for a single page, perform the following steps:

1. Position the cursor somewhere on the page where you want to suppress the page number, header, or footer.

2. Open the **L**ayout menu, choose **P**age, then choose **S**uppress. WordPerfect displays the Suppress dialog box.

3. Under Suppress on Current Page, place an X in all check boxes for page formatting features you don't want to print in the page.

4. Choose the OK button to return to the document.

Exercise 4: Adding Page Numbers to a Document

For this exercise you will place page numbers in a new, blank document.

1. Open a new document.

2. Press ⏎Enter twice to create a couple of blank lines.

3. Press Ctrl + ⏎Enter to create a hard page break.

4. Move the cursor back to the top of the document and add page numbers that are placed at bottom center of each page.

5. View the document with Page view and examine the page numbers.

6. Exit the document without saving.

6.5: To Control Page Breaks

Although word processors in general are very good at determining when to break text and start a new page, sometimes users need to be able to have this control. You have already seen how you can manually enter a hard page break, by pressing Ctrl + ⏎Enter. WordPerfect offers a utility called Widow/Orphan protection that keeps paragraphs from breaking across pages at the very beginning and very end of paragraphs. A *widow* is the last line of a paragraph that appears at the top of a page. An *orphan* is the first line of a paragraph that appears at the bottom of a page, with the remaining text in the paragraph printed on the next page. Widows and orphans are generally considered to be stylistic "mistakes" in most writing style guides.

Using Widow/Orphan Protection

The Widow/Orphan Protection feature can prevent single lines from being "stranded" at the top or bottom of a page. In WordPerfect, a paragraph's first line alone at the bottom of a page is an *orphan*; a paragraph's last line alone at the top of a page is a *widow*.

Turning on Widow/Orphan Protection

 STEPS

To turn on the Widow/Orphan Protection feature, follow these steps:

1. Position the cursor at the place in the document where you want to prevent widows and orphans. To prevent widows and orphans from appearing in the entire document, move the cursor to the beginning of the document.

2. Open the **L**ayout menu, choose **P**age, and then choose **K**eep Text Together.

3. From the Keep Text Together dialog box, place an X in the **P**revent the First and Last Lines of Paragraphs from Being Separated across Pages box.

4. Choose OK to return to the document window.

5. To turn off Widow/Orphan protection at a certain place in the document, open the Keep Text Together dialog box and remove the X from the **P**revent the First and Last Lines of Paragraphs from Being Separated across Pages box.

    WordPerfect inserts a `[Wid/Orph:off]` code that turns off Widow/Orphan protection.

Unit Summary

In this unit, you have learned about page formatting features, including how to change the paper size and top and bottom margins, how to insert headers and footers, how to number pages, and how to control page breaks.

New Terms

To test your knowledge of the new terms in this unit, consult the glossary at the end of this book.

- Footer
- Hard page break
- Header
- Orphan
- Soft page break
- Widow

Testing Your Skills 2

For this Testing Your Skills section, prepare a multi-page paper for a class you are taking this semester. If you don't have a paper due soon, use an article from the local or school newspaper.

Your paper should have the following attributes:

- Be at least 3 pages in length
- Have left margins of 1.5"
- Have right margins of 1"
- Have a header that has your name and student ID number in it
- Have a footer that contains the date the paper is due and the course for which you are doing the paper
- Use bulleted lists, special indents, and enhancement features to format your paper so that it is easy to read.

Turn in a printout and disk copy of the paper.

7

Using WordPerfect's Customizing Features

WordPerfect for Windows offers many functions to help you customize the way in which the program interacts with you. In addition, WordPerfect provides many of the same file maintenance capabilities that Windows usually handles. As a result, you can perform such tasks as deleting, renaming, and copying files from within the WordPerfect program.

This chapter focuses on features that can help you make your system easier to work with and more specific to your needs.

7.1: To Work with Print Options

With WordPerfect, you can print all or part of any document you create. You can print selected text, a range of pages, or the entire document. You also can print more than one copy of a document in a single step. Many of the options available for printing are found in the Print dialog box. By default, WordPerfect prints a single copy of the full document.

It is important to keep in mind the amount of paper you use to print. It is easy to complete a paper and find five or six drafts laying around on the desk. Always proofread your work on screen before sending it to the printer.

Printing the Current Page or Entire Document

To print the current page or entire document, perform the following steps:

1. Open the document that you want to print, or if multiple documents are open, activate the window displaying the document you want printed.

2. Open the File menu, and choose Print. The Print dialog box is displayed (see fig. 7.1).

Fig. 7.1
The Print dialog box.

3. At the top of the Print dialog box, WordPerfect shows the name of the current printer. To switch to a different printer, choose the Select button, and double-click the name of the new printer.

4. To print the current page only, choose the Current Page option button. Full Document, which will print the entire document, is the default.

5. To print multiple copies, enter a new value in the Number of Copies text box.

6. To generate multiple copies of a document with the pages of the document collated during printing, change the setting in the Generated By drop-down list to Printer. (Your printer must have the capability to collate.)

7. To begin printing, choose the Print command button.

When you choose **Print**, WordPerfect displays a message box informing you of the page or pages being sent to the Windows Print Manager. To cancel printing, you must select the Cancel button in this message box before the program sends all of the pages to the Print Manager. As soon as the message box is gone, you can resume working in WordPerfect.

Specifying a Range of Pages to Print

STEPS

To specify particular pages of a document to print, perform the following steps:

1. From the Print dialog box, choose **Multiple Pages**, then choose the **Print** command button. The Multiple Pages dialog box is displayed.

2. Choose the **Pages** command button, and enter the pages you want printed in the Pages text box. The program defaults to All.

3. Choose the **Print** command button.

You can specify different print ranges when using the Multiple Pages dialog box. The following table demonstrates several print ranges that you can enter in the Multiple Pages dialog box, and the pages that are printed.

Print Range Entered	*Pages Printed*
3	3
2,4,6	2, 4 and 6
1 5	1 and 5
2-	Starting at page 2, to the end of the document
2-4	2 through 4

Exercise 1: Exploring Print Options

In this exercise you will simply explore the print options available to you.

1. Start WordPerfect and open a blank document, if necessary.

2. Open the Print dialog box and examine the default settings.

3. What kinds of printers do you have available?

4. Are the number of copies you can make controlled in your computer lab?

5. Return the dialog box to its initial settings and close the dialog box.

7.2: To Understand QuickList

By using QuickList, you can easily identify the directories that contain the document files you frequently need and use. You can assign a descriptive title to any directory or single file to save you from having to remember and type long subdirectory path names. QuickList does not limit you to the standard DOS file-naming practice of eight characters or fewer. You can make the titles for files as long and descriptive as is needed.

Creating a QuickList

To create a QuickList of frequently used files, perform the following steps:

1. Choose a WordPerfect command that uses a Filename list box, such as the **File Open** command.

2. From the Open File dialog box, choose the QuickList command button. The QuickList pop-up menu appears.

3. Choose Show Both to display both the QuickList box and the Directories box in the Open File dialog box.

4. Choose the QuickList command button, then choose **Add** Item from the pop-up menu. The Add QuickList Item dialog box is displayed.

5. In the Directory/Filename field, enter the path and file name you wish to add to the QuickList.

6. Enter a short (a single word is best) description in the **Description** text box.

7. Choose OK to return to the Open File dialog box, where the described item is displayed in the QuickList box.

You could also give an entire directory of files a new descriptive name by typing in the name of the directory in the Directory/ Filename text box.

Editing a QuickList

STEPS

To change the contents of an existing QuickList item or change the descriptive title, perform the following steps:

1. From the QuickList list box in the dialog box, select the QuickList item that you want to change and click the right mouse button (or the QuickList command button). WordPerfect displays the QuickList pop-up menu.

2. Choose Edit Item. WordPerfect displays the Edit QuickList Item dialog box.

3. Type the name of the directory or file name into the Directory/ Filename text box to change the contents of the QuickList item.

4. Enter the changed description into the **Description** text box to change the name of the QuickList item.

5. Choose OK to return to the Open File dialog box. The new changes are displayed in the QuickList box in the Open File dialog box.

Deleting a QuickList Item

STEPS

To remove an existing QuickList item from the QuickList box, perform the following steps:

1. From the dialog box, select the QuickList item that you want to delete, then choose the QuickList command button.

2. Choose Delete Item. WordPerfect for Windows displays a message box for you to confirm the deletion of the selected item from the QuickList.

3. Choose Yes to confirm the deletion and return to the Open File dialog box. The selected item is removed from the QuickList box.

The following options are available when you first choose the QuickList command button from the Open File dialog box:

*   *Show QuickList*. Replaces the Directories list box with a QuickList list box displaying any QuickLists you have defined.

*   *Show Directories*. The default setting which displays a directory tree in the **Directories** list box.

*   *Show Both*. Reduces the default **Directories** list box to a smaller size and adds a QuickList list box above it.

Displaying Files with QuickList

To display files using the QuickList feature, perform the following steps:

1. Choose a WordPerfect command that uses a directories and files dialog box, such as **File Save As**, **File Open**, or **Insert File**.

2. Make sure that the QuickList box is displayed. If not, choose QuickList, and then choose Show QuickList or Show Both.

3. In the QuickList list box, click the descriptive name of the directory or file you want to list in the Filename list box. WordPerfect displays the entire directory path in the Filename box and all the files in that directory in the list box beneath the directory path.

4. Select the file you want to use from the list box, or enter the new file name in the Filename text box.

5. Choose the appropriate command button, such as OK.

6. The dialog box will close and you will be returned to your document.

Exercise 2: Creating a QuickList for Text Exercises

In this exercise you will create a QuickList entry for files created during exercises in this text.

1. Insert your lab work disk, which contains all the files you've done for this text so far, into drive A: and make it the active disk in the Open File dialog box.

2. Make any necessary adjustments, so that both the file list and the QuickList entries show.

3. From the QuickList menu, add the file Calendar.mem with the description: **Text Exercises** to the QuickList.

4. View the result of step 3 in the Open File dialog box.

5. Add the files Board1-9.ltr, Sale.sgn, and Money.ltr to the QuickList with the Text Exercises description as well.

6. Click OK to close the Open File dialog box.

7.3: To Use File Management Options

WordPerfect simplifies common file maintenance chores, such as copying, moving, renaming, or deleting files. You can perform any of these tasks by using the File Options drop-down list box that is located in the Open File, Insert File, and Save As dialog boxes. Choosing File Options from any of these dialog boxes activates a drop-down menu of file management choices (see fig. 7.2).

Fig. 7.2
The drop-down
menu of file
management
choices.

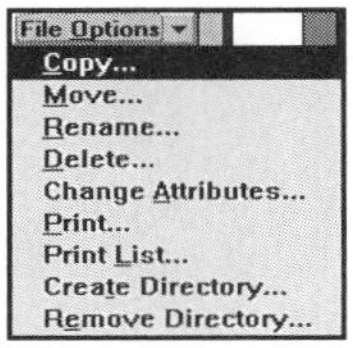

 The following two methods can be used to carry out the commands from the File Options pull-down menu.

NOTE

- Select the name of the file or files from the Filename list box in the Open File, Insert File, or Save As File dialog box.

- Click the File Options button. From the drop-down menu, select a command. When the associated dialog box appears for the selected command, the file name(s) that you have chosen appear in the Filename text box. By using this method, you can select more than one file at a time and save yourself from having to type the file name in the Filename text box.

- Choose the desired command from the File Options drop-down menu. When the associated dialog box appears, type the file name.

The following steps assume that you have used the highlighting method for choosing the desired file name(s) from the list box. You are to use the Open File dialog box to access the File Options pop-up menu.

Copying a File

STEPS

To copy a file by using the File Options drop-down menu, perform the following steps:

1. In the Open File dialog box, select a file name from the File list box.

2. Choose the File Options command button, and then choose Copy.

   WordPerfect displays the Copy File dialog box. The To and From text boxes display the default path, directory, and file name of the file to be copied.

3. The file you selected in step 1 should appear in the From box.

4. In the To text box, type **the new file name/drive letter**.

5. If you check the Don't Replace Files with the Same Size, Date, and Time box, WordPerfect assigns the current date, time, and file size to the new copy.

6. Choose Copy to perform the copy and return to the Open File dialog box.

7. Close the Open File dialog box.

Deleting a File

To delete a file using the File Options drop-down list, perform the following steps:

1. Highlight the name of the file you wish to delete in the File list box.

2. Choose the File Options command button and choose Delete. WordPerfect displays the Delete File dialog box with the selected file included in the text box (see fig. 7.3).

 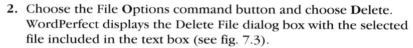 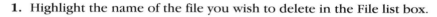

Fig. 7.3
The Delete File dialog box.

3. Choose Delete to delete the selected file or directory and return to the previous Open File dialog box. The deleted file is removed from the file list in the Open File dialog box.

 Be careful when using the Delete command. WordPerfect does not prompt you before deleting the file.

Printing a List of Files

To print a list of files using the File Options pull-down list, perform the following steps:

1. Choose Print List. The Print File List dialog box is displayed.

2. If you choose more than one file for the file list, WordPerfect chooses the Print List of Selected Files command button.

3. If you don't choose any files in the Filename list box, or choose just one, WordPerfect chooses the Print Entire List button.

4. Choose **Print** to begin printing after choosing either selection.

To Create a Directory

To create a new subdirectory using the File Options pull-down list, follow these steps:

1. Choose Create Directory. WordPerfect displays the Create Directory dialog box (see fig. 7.4).

Fig. 7.4
The Create
Directory
dialog box.

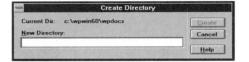

2. Type the name and path for the new directory in the New Directory text box.

3. Choose **Create** to return to the previous dialog box.

To Remove a Directory

To remove a subdirectory using the File Options pull-down list, do the following:

1. Choose Remove Directory. The Remove Directory dialog box is displayed, with the current directory listed in the Directory Text box (see fig. 7.5).

Fig. 7.5
The Remove
Directory
dialog box.

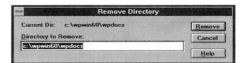

2. Accept the current directory name in the **D**irectory text box, or type the name of the directory you want removed.

3. Choose **Remove**. If the directory contains files, WordPerfect displays a message box warning that the specified directory contains files. You must choose **Yes** or **No** to confirm the removal of the directory. If the directory contains subdirectories, WordPerfect displays a message box warning that the specified directory contains files and subdirectories. You must choose **Yes** or **No** to confirm the removal of the directory.

4. Choose **Yes** to remove files from directories or subdirectories from within directories, or choose **No** to cancel the process.

Additional options in the File Options drop-down menu include

- *Print*. Prints a selected file.
- *Change Attributes*. Enables you to change the attributes of a file. You can use the **Read-Only** option to save a file and prevent yourself or others from making changes to the file. The **Archive** option (the default) saves the file as an archived file.
- *Rename*. Replaces an existing file name with a different name.
- *Move*. Enables you to move a file from one location (drive, directory) to another.

Exercise 3: Managing Files with File Options

1. In this exercise you will make a backup of one of the lab files and create a new directory on your floppy disk.

2. Make sure your floppy disk in drive A: is the active disk.

3. Create a new directory, using the File Options menu, called **Labbak** on the floppy disk.

4. Copy the file Calendar.mem in the LABBAK subdirectory to a file called Calendar.bak.

7.4: To Use Preferences to Change Defaults

You can customize many WordPerfect program features by using the **Preferences** option on the **File** menu. The features activated by this command enable you to change the program defaults—the way WordPerfect behaves and displays information every time you use the program. The changes you make in the Preferences dialog box affect the documents you create in the future, not just the current document.

If you are computing in a public computing facility such as a computer lab or classroom, you should not attempt to do this section. **WARNING** Most system administrators lock end users out of the preferences so that they cannot make changes which will damage or destroy the computing environment. If you are working in a shared computing environment, simply be aware of some of the changes you could make to the preferences if you were working on your own machine.

Customizing the Status Bar

STEPS

You can customize many aspects of WordPerfect's screen display with the options in the Display Preferences dialog box. To change the way information appears in the status bar, perform the following steps:

1. Open the File menu, and choose Preferences. WordPerfect displays the Preferences menu (see fig. 7.6).

Fig. 7.6
The Preferences
menu.

2. Choose Status Bar. The Status Bar Preferences dialog box is displayed (see fig. 7.7).

Fig. 7.7
The Status Bar
Preferences
dialog box.

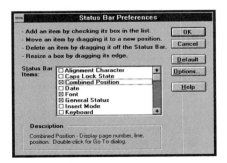

3. To add new items to the status bar, place an X next to the desired options in the **S**tatus Bar Items list box by clicking the check box beside the item. To remove an option, click the box again so that the X is removed.

4. To resize an item on the status bar, position the mouse pointer on one of the item's edges. When the pointer is a double-headed arrow, drag to the left or right to decrease or increase the item's size. The Status Bar Preferences dialog box must be displayed when you do this.

5. To rearrange the items on the status bar, drag the item's outline with the mouse to the new position.

6. To change the appearance of information in each item or the item itself on the status bar, choose the **O**ptions button.

7. Select a new font, font size, or other appearance option; then choose OK to return to the Status Bar Preferences dialog box.

8. Choose OK to see the changes take effect.

9. To return the status bar to the default setting, choose the **D**efault button in the Status Bar Preferences dialog box.

Displaying the Ruler Bar in All Document Windows

To make WordPerfect automatically display the Ruler Bar in all document windows that you open, perform the following steps:

1. Open the **F**ile menu; then choose P**r**eferences. WordPerfect displays the Preferences dialog box.

2. Double-click the **D**isplay option. WordPerfect displays the Display Preferences dialog box.

3. Choose the **R**uler Bar option button. The bottom half of the Display Preferences dialog box displays options for the Ruler Bar command button (see fig. 7.8).

4. Choose Sho**w** Ruler on New and Current Document so that an X appears in the check box.

5. Choose OK to return to the document screen.

Fig. 7.8
The Display
Preferences dialog
box with the Ruler
Bar option button
selected.

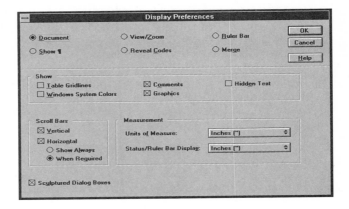

Displaying the Reveal Codes Window in All Document Windows

 STEPS

To make WordPerfect automatically display the Reveal Codes window in all document windows that you open, perform the following steps:

1. Open the File menu, choose Preferences, and then choose Display. WordPerfect displays the Display Preferences dialog box.

2. Choose the Reveal Codes option button.

3. Choose Show Reveal Codes on New and Current Document so that an X appears in the check box. You can also modify such things as the font and font size shown in the codes by placing an X in the appropriate check box.

7.5: To Customize the Way File Names Are Displayed

You can customize the way WordPerfect for Windows displays file names in the Open File dialog box. For example, you can sort files in a number of different ways, show only certain elements of the file listing, or place the elements in Custom Columns. The following list describes the different options available under Setup in the Open File dialog box.

- *Show*. From this option, you can choose Filename Only; Filename, Size, Date, Time; Descriptive Name, Filename; or Custom Columns.

To Customize the Way File Names Are Displayed

NOTE

If you choose **Custom Columns**, WordPerfect displays the file name, size, date, and time in the Open File dialog box. You then can rearrange the order of the columns by dragging the column titles with the mouse (see figure 7.9). The Show Column Labels check box, located in the Open/Save As Setup dialog box, must be checked to reorder the columns.

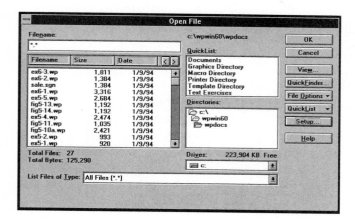

Fig. 7.9
The File list box displaying files in Custom Columns.

- *Sort By*. To tell WordPerfect how to sort the file display, choose this option. Then choose **Filename**, **Extension**, **Size**, **Date/Time**, Descriptive **Name**, or Descriptive **Type** as the basis of the sort.
- *Sort Order*. Choose this option, and then choose **Ascending** (the default) or **Descending** to have WordPerfect sort files accordingly.
- *Change Default Directory*. Choosing this option makes a directory selected in the Open File dialog box **Directories** list box the default directory.
- *List Files of Type*. Choose this option to display a specific file type; for example, to display only files with a DOC extension. All Files is the default setting.

Exercise 4: Using Custom Columns to Display File Names

In this exercise you will modify the setup dialog box so that custom columns show.

1. Select **File Open** from the menu.

2. From the File Open dialog box, select **Setup**.

3. Pull down the Show option list and select Custom Columns.

4. In the Sort By field, select Date/Time.

5. In the Sort Order field, selection Descending.

6. If Create Speedup Files is selected, deselect it.

7. Click OK and view the results in the File Open dialog box.

8. Quit WordPerfect at this time or continue with the next unit.

Unit Summary

In this unit, you learned the many ways to customize WordPerfect features. You learned how to change options when printing, how to use the QuickList and Preferences features, and how to change the display of file listings in the Open File dialog box.

New Terms

To check your knowledge of the new terms in this unit, consult the Glossary at the end of this book.

- Document summary
- QuickList
- Archive attribute

Merging Documents

The Merge feature (often referred to as *mail merge*) represents one of WordPerfect's most versatile tools. You use the Merge feature to insert variable information into a standard format. In this unit, you learn to use the Merge feature to create personalized form letters, to address envelopes, and to create mailing labels.

8.1: To Create Files to Merge

A merge operation involves two files: a *form file* (primary file) and a *data file* (secondary file). The form file is a skeleton document containing merge codes and text that remains the same for each copy of the document produced by the merge operation.

The data file consists of variable information, which is organized into fields and records. An example of a data file is an employee. All the information relating to one employee within the data file is called a *record*. Each record contains data items, called fields. Fields in the employee list can include such information as first name, last name, company, address, city, state, and ZIP code.

By matching the merge codes you have placed in both the form and data merge files, WordPerfect determines which fields in the data file are used and where the information is inserted in the form file during the merge process. When combined with the form file, each record in the data file produces a different document.

Objectives

When you have finished with this unit you will have learned the following:

8.1 To Create Files to Merge

8.2 To Create a Form File

8.3 To Merge Form and Data Files

Creating a Text Data File

When creating a data file, you must make sure that every record in the file has the same number of fields and that the fields are in the same order in all records. At times, you may not have information to include in a field for a record; however, you must still include the field in the record even though the field is blank. If you skip a field in a record because of missing information or if you mix up your entries and place them in the wrong fields, WordPerfect will merge incorrect information into the form file.

STEPS

To create a text data file, perform the following steps:

1. Open a new document window.

2. Open the Tools menu, and choose Merge. WordPerfect displays the Merge dialog box (see fig. 8.1).

Fig. 8.1
The Merge
dialog box.

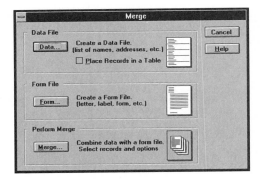

3. To create a text data file, make sure that the **P**lace Records in a Table check box is not marked.

4. Choose the **D**ata button to open the Create Data File dialog box. WordPerfect displays the Create Data File dialog box.

5. Type the name for the first field in the **N**ame a Field text box. WordPerfect inserts the name into the **F**ield Name List box.

6. Continue to type the field names into the text box, pressing ⏎Enter after each entry.

7. When you are finished entering all of the fields, choose the OK button to close the Create Data File dialog box.

Exercise 1: Creating the Data File

In this exercise you will create the data file structure that will be used in subsequent exercises in this unit.

1. Start WordPerfect and open a new document if you haven't already done so.

2. Make the appropriate menu selections to open the Create Data File dialog box.

3. Create fields for the following items:

   Company

   Street

   City

   State

   ZIP

   First Name

4. Click OK. WordPerfect automatically displays the Quick Data Entry dialog box that you use to enter the records for the new data file (see fig. 8.2). This dialog box contains a text box for each field you have defined.

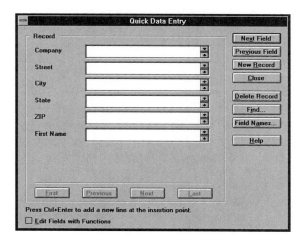

Fig. 8.2
The Quick Data
Entry dialog box.

Entering Information in a Data File

To enter data for your records into the Quick Data Entry dialog box, type the information for each field into its corresponding text box, then press Tab⁺ or Next to move to the next field.

Exercise 2: Entering Data

In this exercise you will enter data into the Quick Data Entry dialog box. The Quick Data Entry dialog box should be on-screen before you begin this exercise. You will use this data file in subsequent exercises in this unit.

1. Type **Interior Design Inc.** in the Company text box.

2. Press Tab⁺ or click the Next Field button to move to the next line.

3. Type **123 Brown St.** in the Street text box, and press Tab⁺.

4. Type **Chicago** in the City text box, and press Tab⁺.

5. Type **IL** in the State text box, and press Tab⁺.

6. Type **60611** in the ZIP text box, and press Tab⁺.

7. Type **James** in the First Name text box, and then choose New **Record** to clear the text boxes so that you can make the entries for the next record.

8. Enter the following information in the appropriate fields for the next three records.

Company	Computerland Inc.	ABC Company	Fashion Trends
Street	711 Madison St.	301 North Pl.	6550 Oak St.
City	San Francisco	Valparaiso	Phoenix
State	CA	IN	AZ
ZIP	94107	46383	66343
First Name	Bob	Jason	Norma

9. When you have finished entering the information for these records, choose the Close button. WordPerfect asks whether you want to save the changes to disk.

10. Choose **Yes**, and save the file as **A:CUST.DAT**. The data file and the Merge feature bar are displayed in the document window (see fig. 8.3).

Editing Records in the Data File

You can edit existing records by using the Quick Data Entry dialog box. To edit an existing record, perform the following steps:

1. Click the **Quick Entry** button on the Merge Feature bar. The Quick Data Entry dialog box is displayed (refer to fig. 8.2).

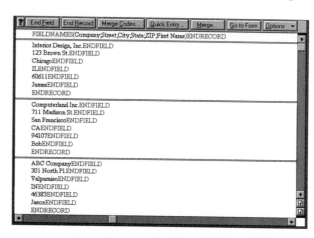

Fig. 8.3
WordPerfect displays the data file and Merge feature bar in the document window.

2. Use the **First**, **Previous**, **Next**, and **Last** buttons to move through the records in the data file.

3. Use the **Find** button to locate a specific record in the data file by searching for specific information in one of its fields. Choose Find. WordPerfect displays the Find Text dialog box.

4. Enter the text for which you want to search.

5. Choose **Options** from the dialog box menu; choose **Begin** Find at Top of Document.

6. Choose **Match** from the dialog box menu and select criteria for matching found text.

   a. **Whole word** matches only whole words (e.g., if you search for IN, it won't match Interior, only the state abbreviation IN, since it is a complete word).

   b. **Case** matches the case of each letter you enter to the case in the text. If you enter SMITH, WordPerfect will not find Smith.

   c. **Font** finds matches based on font.

   d. **Codes** matches WordPerfect's hidden codes.

7. When you have finished making the Find settings, choose the **Find Next** button. In the Quick Data Entry dialog box, WordPerfect displays the first record containing text that matches the search text.

8. Press `Tab⇥` to move to the field you wish to change.

9. Make any necessary changes.

10. Choose New **Record**.

11. To find another record with the same text, choose **Find** from the Quick Data Entry dialog box. WordPerfect displays the Find Text dialog box, containing the record information for which you last searched.

12. Choose the **Find Next** button in the Find Text dialog box. When WordPerfect cannot find another match, it stays on the last matching record found.

13. Choose OK.

14. Choose the **Close** button in the Quick Data Entry dialog box after making any editing changes. WordPerfect records the change and displays a message box asking whether you want to save your changes to disk.

15. Choose **Yes**. WordPerfect displays the Save As dialog box. Choose OK. WordPerfect displays another dialog box warning you that you are about to replace an existing data file with the modified file.

16. Choose **Yes** again to save the changes.

17. Open the **File** menu, and choose **Close** to return to a blank document screen.

Exercise 3: Editing a Record

In this exercise you will locate a record and change the address.

1. With the Cust.dat file open, find the record with the address 301 North Pl.

2. When the record has been located, edit the address so that it reads **444 North Pl**.

3. Close the database and replace the existing database with the modified database.

4. Close the file completely so that you have a blank document screen in front of you.

8.2: To Create a Form File

The form file contains the document text plus FIELD merge codes that indicate which data items are to be used from the data file. In addition to the FIELD codes, you may want to insert the DATE merge code into the form file so that when you perform the merge, WordPerfect automatically replaces the DATE code with the current date.

To create a letter form file to be merged with the data file, perform the following steps:

1. Open the **Tools** menu; then choose **Merge**. WordPerfect displays the Merge dialog box (refer to fig. 8.1).

2. Choose the **Form** button. The Create Form File dialog box appears.

3. In the **Associate a Data File** text box, enter the file name of the data file that you will be using and choose OK. A new document screen appears, into which you will enter the fields and text of your form letter.

4. Position the cursor at the top of the document.

5. Insert the DATE code into the text of the form letter by clicking the **Date** button on the Merge Feature Bar.

6. Press ⏎Enter twice to skip a line and position the cursor where you want to begin entering additional information.

7. Click the **Insert Field** button on the Merge Feature Bar to access the Insert Field Name or Number dialog box (see fig. 8.4).

Fig. 8.4
The Insert Field Name or Number dialog box.

8. Highlight the desired field, choose the **Insert** button, and press ⏎Enter to move down a line. When you choose the **Insert** button, WordPerfect inserts a FIELD merge code at the cursor's position in the form document. This FIELD code contains the name of the field.

9. Insert the desired fields.

When placing codes in the form file, remember that you must insert any spaces or punctuation needed to separate the fields.

10. When you are finished typing the letter, choose **Close** to exit the Insert Field Name or Number box.

11. Open the **File** menu, and choose **Close**. WordPerfect asks whether you want to save the file.

12. Choose **Yes**, and give the file a name.

Exercise 4: Creating the Letter

In this exercise you will create the boilerplate letter for the merge.

1. In a blank document, make the appropriate menu selections to open a merge form.

2. Place the **Date** code at the top of the document and press ⏎Enter twice.

3. Insert the code for the Company field and press ⏎Enter.

4. Insert the code for the Street field and press ⏎Enter.

5. Insert the code for the City field, and type , (comma). Press Spacebar.

6. Insert the field for State and press Spacebar twice.

7. Insert the field for ZIP and press ⏎Enter twice.

8. Type **Dear** and insert the field for First Name, followed by a : (colon).

9. Enter the remaining portion of the letter, shown in figure 8.5.

Fig. 8.5
The form file for
a standard form
letter.

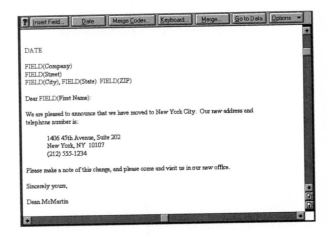

10. When the letter has been entered, save the file as **Cust.frm** and close the document.

8.3: To Merge Form and Data Files

After you have created the form and data files, you can perform the merge. You can merge the files to the current document, to a new document window, directly to the printer, or to an existing disk file. By default, the program separates the merged documents with hard page returns, prints one copy of each merged document, and leaves a blank line in the merged document when it encounters an empty field in a record.

Performing a Typical Merge

To merge the data file and form file, perform the following steps:

1. Open the File menu, and choose Open.

2. Enter the name of the form file you want to use in the merge operation.

3. Choose OK.

4. From the Merge Feature Bar, choose Merge. WordPerfect displays the Merge dialog box.

5. Choose the Merge button. WordPerfect displays the Perform Merge dialog box (see fig. 8.6).

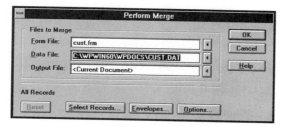

Fig. 8.6
The Perform
Merge dialog box.

In the Perform Merge dialog box, you indicate the files you want to merge, as well as choose the merge options.

6. Check the files listed in the Files to Merge text boxes. If they are incorrect, you can type the correct form file name, data file name, and output file name.

7. Choose the OK button to close the Perform Merge dialog box and perform the merge. WordPerfect displays a Please Wait message box indicating which records are being merged.

8. Examine the merged documents in the new document window by scrolling toward the beginning of the document.

9. To save the merged documents, open the File menu, and choose the Save command. Give a new name to the merged document. It is common practice to give all merged documents the file extension .mer, to denote that the file is the result of a merge.

When the file you are merging is a large document, you may want to send it directly to the printer instead of sending it to the screen. Large files that are merged and sent to the screen use up a great deal of memory, which can be a problem if your computer has a limited amount of memory.

The following options are available in the Perform Merge dialog box:

- *Form File*. <Current Document> The current active document will be used as the form file unless otherwise specified using a different file name.

- *Data file*. The file name of the data file that is to be used with the current form file.

- *Output File*. <New Document> You can merge files to the current document or a new document, directly to the printer, or to an existing disk file (which you can print at a later time).

- *Select Records*. Choose this option to limit the merge to certain records by marking records or specifying conditions.

- *Envelope*. Choose this option to create envelopes as you merge your document. The envelopes are added to the end of the merged file.

- *Options*. Choose this option to control the appearance of the merged file. For example, you can separate each merged document with a page break, specify the number of copies of each record in the data file to print multiple copies of each merged document, and eliminate blank lines when there is a blank field in the data file.

Exercise 5: Merging the Cust Files

In this exercise you will merge the Cust.dat and Cust.frm files.

1. Clear the screen of any open documents, leaving only a blank, untitled document open.

2. Make the appropriate menu selections to perform a merge.

3. In the Perform Merge dialog box, enter the appropriate file name in each field.

4. Click OK when you are ready to merge.

5. Examine the merged records. Each letter should be "personalized" and separated from the next letter by a hard page break.

6. Save the merged file as **Cust.mer**.

Selecting the Records to Merge

You can select certain records from a data file to be used in the merge operation. You can mark the records individually, designate a range of records, or specify a selection condition that must be met before the records are used.

Marking Records Individually

To select records individually for a merge by using the marking method, follow these steps:

1. Open the Perform Merge dialog box.

2. Choose Select Records. WordPerfect displays the Select Records dialog box (see fig. 8.7).

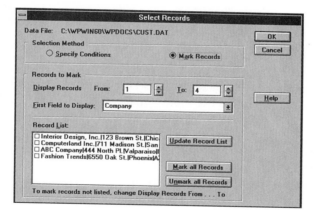

Fig. 8.7
The Select Records dialog box with the Mark Records option selected.

3. Choose the Mark Records option. The Select Records dialog box displays part of the first set of records in the Record List box.

4. From the Record List box, select the records that you want to include in the merge by clicking the inside of the box to place an X in it.

5. To control which records are displayed when making your selections, choose the Display Records From option, and enter the starting record number. Enter the ending record number into the To text box.

6. Choose the First Field to Display option, and select the field name from the drop-down list to change the first field displayed in the Record List box.

7. Choose Update Record List button to show the range of records and the first field displayed. After selecting the records you want to include, choose OK.

Selecting a Range of Record Numbers

To select a range of record numbers to include in a merge operation, follow these steps:

1. Open the Perform Merge dialog box. The Specify Conditions button is selected by default.

2. Choose Select Records; then choose Record Number Range.

3. Enter the first record number to include in the From text box, and the last record number to include in the To text box.

4. Choose OK.

Unit Summary

In this unit, you learned about WordPerfect's Merge features. You learned how to merge a data file and a form file and how to select only certain records for the merged file. You also learned how to create mailing labels.

New Terms

To check your knowledge of the new terms in this unit, consult the Glossary at the end of this book.

- Data file
- Field
- Form file
- Merge
- Record

Testing Your Skills 3

You have decided to apply for summer jobs. Now that you're a WordPerfect whiz, you know that you can create professional-looking letters that will impress your future employer.

Locate three businesses in your town at which you would like to work. Create a data file called **Jobs.dat** with each business's company name, address, city, state, and ZIP code. If you have a contact person at that business, also create a salutation name field (like Ms. Jones). Enter data for the three businesses that you have selected.

Create a data form to introduce yourself and the special skills you believe you could bring to the business. Your letter should contain a date code, and merge fields for each field in the Jobs.dat data file. Your letter should be honest and well-written. Remember, you're trying to get your foot in the corporate door with this letter. Name the file **Jobs.frm**.

Merge the Jobs.dat and Jobs.frm files. Check for any errors and make any necessary corrections. Save the file as **Jobs.mer**. Print the letters.

Finally, refer to Unit 3, "Using the Coaches," to learn how to create envelopes for each prospective business. Attach the envelopes to the Jobs.mer file. Save the file one last time.

Glossary

Antonym. A word that has the opposite or nearly opposite meaning of another word. When you choose a headword in WordPerfect's Thesaurus, you are shown lists of antonyms as well as synonyms.

Archive attribute. Causes a file to be backed up the next time you run a backup program.

Click. To press and then immediately release the mouse button.

Clipboard. An area of computer memory that holds the text or graphics you cut or copy. You can paste from the Clipboard into different documents in WordPerfect or into different applications.

Copy. To duplicate selected text or graphics. When you choose the Copy command from the Edit menu, WordPerfect for Windows places a copy of the selected item in the Clipboard. When you combine copying with pasting, you can copy text from one location to another.

Cursor (insertion point). The flashing vertical marker that indicates where the next character will be inserted when you type. To move the cursor, use the cursor movement keys or position the I-beam pointer in the text, and click the left mouse button.

Cut. To remove selected text or graphics from a document. When you choose the Cut command from the Edit menu, WordPerfect for Windows removes the selected item from the document and stores it in the Clipboard. When performing cut-and-paste operations, you can move text from one location to another.

Data file. A file containing the variable data or individual data items that are merged into the primary merge file. These data items are organized into a rigid format of fields and records.

Dialog box. A box that WordPerfect for Windows displays whenever additional information is needed in order to complete a task.

Dictionary. A file named WP{WP}US.LEX, which contains about 115,000 words that WordPerfect uses to check your documents for spelling errors. When checking spelling, WordPerfect ignores all words that are spelled correctly according to this dictionary.

Document summary. Brief description of the contents and vital statistics about a document. This information can help you quickly identify and locate the document later on.

Document window. A smaller window within the WordPerfect program window. A document window contains each open document. WordPerfect for Windows enables you to have open as many as nine documents at a time.

Double-click. To press and release the mouse button twice in rapid succession.

Drag. To hold down the left mouse button while moving the mouse across an area, such as a desk or mouse pad.

Field. A basic unit of information that makes up a record in a secondary merge file. Each field contains the same type of information, such as the company name, address, city, state, and ZIP code.

File name. A descriptive name you give your document when you save it. The file name can contain up to eight characters with a three-character extension and is always displayed in the title bar.

Font. A collection of characters with an identifiable typeface, such as Courier or Times Roman. In WordPerfect, you can assign fonts from the Ruler, the Font menu, or the Font dialog box.

Footer. Text that is automatically printed at the bottom of every page of the document.

Form file. A skeleton document containing the fixed format into which data items are merged.

Hard page break. A page break that you manually insert into the document. A hard page break appears as a double dashed line across the document window.

Hard return. The code that WordPerfect inserts when you press ⏎Enter to end a paragraph of text.

Header. Text that is automatically printed at the top of every page of the document.

Headword. A word in the WordPerfect Thesaurus that contains a list of synonyms and antonyms.

Icons. Symbols that represent a program, file, or function. An icon's graphic indicates its function. WordPerfect for Windows uses a special set of icons on the Button Bar; you can click these icons to choose commands.

Insert mode. WordPerfect's default editing mode. New text is inserted at the cursor's position, and existing text moves to the right.

Insertion point. A flashing vertical bar displayed on-screen that indicates where the text you type is placed.

Line height. The amount of space that WordPerfect assigns between lines, measured from the bottom of one line to the bottom of the next.

Merge. To assemble a document by inserting variable data into a fixed format.

Orphan. In WordPerfect, the first line of a paragraph that appears alone at the bottom of a page.

Paste. To place the contents of the Clipboard into a document. After you have copied or cut selected text from a document, you can paste that text into another location.

QuickList. A feature that enables you to assign a descriptive alias to a directory to help you quickly locate its contents.

Record. A collection of fields containing related information pertaining to a single entity, such as the record for a particular company or person.

Ruler. An on-screen tool you use to control paragraph and character formatting, such as tab settings, margin settings, line spacing, justification, fonts, and styles.

Select. To highlight text using the mouse or keyboard so that WordPerfect can identify the text on which you want to perform the next operation.

Soft page break. A page break that WordPerfect automatically inserts into a document. A soft page break appears as a single dashed line across the document window.

Soft return. The code that WordPerfect inserts at the end of a line after word wrap occurs.

String. A collection of characters, including codes and spaces, that WordPerfect uses when executing search and replace operations.

Style. A group of predefined formatting commands that you apply to text by using the mouse or keyboard. When you edit a style, WordPerfect for Windows reformats your document automatically.

Synonym. A word that has an identical or similar meaning to another word. You can use WordPerfect's Thesaurus to look up synonyms for any headword.

Typeover mode. An alternative to Insert mode in which new text replaces existing text.

Widow. In WordPerfect, the last line of a paragraph that appears alone at the top of a page.

Windows. A graphical user interface (GUI) built on the DOS operating system that provides a common user access (CUA) to all the applications that run under it.

Word wrap. The word processing feature that automatically moves a word to the beginning of the next line if the word won't fit within the current margin settings. With word wrap, you need to press ⏎Enter only at the end of a paragraph.

WordPerfect program window. The framed on-screen area that contains the WordPerfect program. The program window contains the title bar, the menu bar, the Power Bar, all currently opened document windows, and the status bar.

Index

Index

Index

Index

H

hanging indent, 67
hard hyphens, 75
hard page break, 121
hard return, 18, 122
hard spaces, 75
Header/Footer options, 84
Header/Footer commands (Layout menu), 83
headers, 82, 122
  adding, 85-86
  creating, 83-84
  editing, 85
  printing, 85
  suppressing, 88-89
Headers/Footers dialog box, 83
headwords (Thesaurus), 53-54, 122
Help, 39-41
Help menu commands
  Coach, 40-41
  Contents, 39
hidden codes, 43-44
History button (Help), 40
hyphenation, 74-76

I

icons, 122
Include Headers, Footers, Etc. option (Find Text dialog box), 46
indenting paragraphs, 65-68
Insert File dialog box, 98
Insert menu commands, 33
Insert mode, 21, 122
inserting
  blank lines in text, 36
  documents in documents, 33-34
  files in files, 33
insertion point, 10, 18, 120-122
italic attribute (Appearance box), 72

J-K

justification, 67-68

key combinations, 7, 20-21
keyboard, 9-11
  alphanumeric keys, 9-10
  Backspace key, 22
  cursor-movement keys, 9-10
  Delete key, 22
  function keys, 9
  navigating text, 19-20
  numeric keys, 9
  pull-down menus, 10
  viewing document summary, 11

L

Landscape mode (paper), 78-80
Layout menu commands
  Envelope, 80
  Font, 71
  Header/Footer, 83
  Line, 69
  Margins, 81
  Page, 78, 81
  Paragraph, 66
Left justification, 67
left margins, 61
left tabs, 63
legal paper (size list), 78
letters, 113
letter paper (size list), 78
Limit Find Within Selection option (Find Text dialog box), 46
Line (Header/Footer bar), 84
line breaks
  controlling, 74-76
  hard spaces, 75
  hyphenating, 74
Line command (Layout menu), 69
line height, 122
line spacing, 73-74

P

page breaks, 89-90
  hard page break, 121
  soft page breaks, 122
Page command (Layout menu), 78, 81
Page mode, 22-24
pages
  printing, 93-94
  numbering, 86-89
Pages (Speller option), 50
paper, 77-80
Paragraph command (Layout menu), 66
paragraphs
  indenting, 65-68
  selecting, 35
Paragraphs (Speller option), 50
Paste command (Edit menu), 38
pasting (text), 30-34, 38-39, 122
percentage option button, 24
Perform Merge dialog box, 115
phonetics (Speller), 49-53
Placement (Header/Footer bar), 84
placement dialog box, 84
points (fonts), 71
Portrait mode (paper), 78
POS indicator (status bar), 18-26
Position After option (Find Text dialog box), 46
Position Before option (Find Text dialog box), 46
Power bar, 3, 7
Preferences command (File menu), 8, 101-104
Previous (Header/Footer bar), 84
Previous button (Undelete dialog box), 37
primary file (form file), 107-112
Print (File Options drop-down menu), 101
Print button (Help), 40

Print command (File menu), 25-26, 93
Print dialog box, 92-95
Print Envelope (envelope option), 79
Print File List dialog box, 99
print options, 92-95
print ranges, 94
Print Return Address (envelope option), 79
printers
  fonts, 72
  switching, 93
printing
  cancelling, 94
  current page, 93-94
  documents, 25-26, 93-94
  files, 26
  footers, 85
  headers, 85
  lists, 99-100
  page ranges, 94
Program Manager, 2
proportionally spaced fonts, 70-71
pull-down menus
  cancelling, 7
  opening, 10
  selecting, 6
punctuation (form files), 113

Q

Quick Data Entry dialog box, 110
QuickFinder (Open File dialog box), 28
QuickLists, 122
  creating, 95-98
  editing, 96
QuickMenus
  Button Bar, 7
  commands
    Clear All Tabs, 64
    selecting, 8

mouse, 6-9
Power Bar, 7
scroll bars, 7
status bar, 7

R

ranges (pages)
printing, 94
selecting, 118-119
rearranging document window, 31-32
records, 122
data files, 107, 111-112, 117
editing, 111-114
fields, 107
ranges, 117-119
selecting, 117-118
removing
directories, 100-101
files, 100-101
formatting symbols, 24
Rename (File Options drop-down menu), 101
renaming
directories, 95
documents, 25
repeating keys, 22
Replace All option (Find and replace Text dialog), 49
Replace command (Edit menu), 48
Replace option (Find and Replace text dialog box), 48
Replace With Text box (Speller window), 51-52
replacement strings, 48
replacing text, 36, 48-49
in Thesaurus, 53
Typeover mode, 21
with Speller, 50
see also find and replace
resizing document windows, 31-32

Restore button (Undelete dialog box), 37
restoring text, 37
retrieving documents, 14
Return Addresses (envelope option), 79
Reveal Codes, 43-44
Reveal Codes command (View menu), 44, 73
Reveal Codes window, 104-105
Right justification, 67
right margins
aligning, 69
setting, 61
right tabs, 63
right-pointing triangle (commands), 7
ruler, 122
Ruler Bar, 3, 103
Ruler Bar command (View menu), 61
Run command (File menu), 2

S

Save As command (File menu), 24-25
Save As dialog box, 25, 98
Save command (File menu), 25, 116
saving
documents, 24-25
memo files, 25
screen, 3
scroll bars (QuickMenus), 7
Search button (Help), 40
search strings, 48-49, 123
searches (wild-card characters), 47
secondary files (data file), 107-112
Select Match option (Find Text dialog box), 46
Select Record (Perform Merge dialog box), 116
Selected Text (Speller option), 50

Index

selecting
   commands, 8
   data files, 117
   fonts, 71-72
   paper size, 78
   records, 117-118
   ranges, 118-119
   sentences, 35
   text, 34-37, 122
Sentences (Speller options), 50
setting
   margins, 61-65
   pages numbers, 87
   tabs, 63-65
settings (default), 17
shortcuts, 35
Show (Open File dialog box), 104
Show command (View menu), 23
size list (paper), 78
Skip Always command button
   (Speller window), 51
Skip Once command button
   (Speller window), 51
soft hyphen, 75
soft page breaks, 122
soft return, 18, 122
Sort By (Open File dialog box), 105
Sort Order (Open File dialog box),
   105
Specific Codes option (Find Text
   dialog box), 46
Speller, 49-53
   alternative spellings, 50-51
   entering changes, 51-52
   options, 50
   running, 53
Speller command (Tools menu), 50
Speller window, 51
   Add command button, 51
   Close command button, 51
   Options pull-down menu, 52
   Replace With Text box, 51-52

Skip Always command button, 51
Skip Once command button, 51
Standard size (paper), 78-80
standard template, 15-16
starting
   documents, 13-17
   WordPerfect, 1-3
Statistics (Grammatik option), 55
status bar, 3
   customizing, 102-103
   QuickMenus, 7
Status Bar Preferences dialog box,
   102
stopping pages, 88
strings, 44-49
   replacement, 48-49
   searches, 48-49, 123
styles, 123
subdirectories, 100-101
subscripts, 73
superscripts, 73
supplemental dictionaries (Speller),
   49-53
suppressing
   footers, 88-89
   headers, 88-89
   page numbers, 88-89
switching printers, 93
symbols, formatting, 23-24
synonyms (Thesaurus), 53, 123

T

Tab Set dialog box, 65
tabs
   changing, 64
   dot leaders, 63
   setting, 65
Template command (File menu), 16
templates
   memo-style letter, 17
   opening, 16
   standard, 15

Index